CHAPEL HILL MURDER & MAYHEM

RICK JACKSON

THE History PRESS

Published by The History Press
Charleston, SC
www.historypress.com

Cover images courtesy of the University of North Carolina Library.

First published 2023

Manufactured in the United States

ISBN 9781467153355

Library of Congress Control Number: 2022947093

For Abraham and my brother, Chris, whose grief is beyond comprehension and known only to him and God.

And even in our sleep, pain which cannot forget falls drop by drop
upon the heart, until in our own despair, against our will,
comes wisdom through the awful grace of God.

—Aeschylus

CONTENTS

INTRODUCTION

On October 17, 1993, in the presence of thousands of alumni and students of the University of North Carolina (UNC) at Chapel Hill, the university's president and staff, the governor of North Carolina and the president of the United States, Charles Kuralt stepped up to the podium and looked around at the sea of Carolina blue. Kenan Stadium, where the UNC Tarheel football team plays, was packed for the bicentennial celebration of the opening of the nation's first public university.

Kuralt was born in Wilmington, North Carolina, and was raised in Charlotte. He was a North Carolinian through and through. He came to Chapel Hill in 1951, as many young people had before him—and have since—to earn what is still one of the finest educations in the world. Upon graduating in 1955, he set out on a media career that would make him an icon. By the time he stood there at the podium in 1993, he was one of the most recognizable people in the United States. From 1967 to 1988, he traveled the country in a small mobile home, interviewing everyday people to get the tone of the nation for the segment "On the Road," which aired on CBS news. He became the first host for *CBS News Sunday Morning* until he retired in 1994.

On that October night, Kuralt looked around at so many people who had started their life journeys into adulthood there with him so many years ago and at the faces of so many young people just starting their own journeys. He greeted the many presidents in attendance, including University President Bill Friday and President Bill Clinton. He greeted Governor Jim Hunt and

University welcome sign. *Author's collection.*

Chancellor Hardin before starting his speech. "I speak for all of us who could not afford to go to Duke." The crowd erupted in laughter and applause at his dig at the school's main rival, the dark blue–loving private institution just eight miles to the east. When the applause died down, he continued, "And would not have, even if we could have afforded it." Once again, the applause and the cheers rang out for young and old throughout the stadium as if a touchdown had just been scored to win the big game.

As the cheers died down again, Kuralt spoke words that have been repeated in videos and university materials that try to encapsulate the feelings of everyone who has ever attended the university—words for the ages. "What is it that binds us to this place as to no other? It is not the well, or the bell, or the stone walls, or the crisp October nights, or the memory of dogwoods blooming....No, our love for this place is based on the fact that it is, as it was meant to be, the university of the people." Nothing else has ever been written or spoken that has brought the beautiful campus to life for so many, whether they attended the university or didn't.

There are few places in the world as serene or lovely as Chapel Hill, North Carolina. The small town and the university have always been one and the

The Old Well at the University of North Carolina stands as the most recognizable symbol of the town and the university across the world. *Author's collection.*

same. Even as the university has grown, the town has been able to maintain the small-town feel that has endeared it to so many students over the years.

The town is named after New Hope Chapel, which was built in 1795 on the site where the Carolina Inn stands today. The University of North Carolina was chartered in 1789 and began to admit students in 1795. The university is one of three that can claim to be the first public university founded in the United States under the Constitution. William and Mary was chartered in 1693 but did not become a public university until 1906. The University of Georgia was chartered in 1785 but did not begin to accept students until 1801. So UNC, although it was chartered later than the University of Georgia, began to admit students several years earlier and is without a doubt the oldest public university still serving students.

The village of Chapel Hill grew up around the school to support the students and staff. As the university grew, so did the town. Since the very beginning of the university's existence, UNC and Chapel Hill have been known as liberal bastions in the middle of the mostly conservative South. Throughout the history of the school and town, they have been more progressive than their neighbors. At times, Chapel Hill was referred to as

The Old Well, pictured here in 1892, was the main source of drinking water on campus for many years. *University of North Carolina Library.*

The Old Well, South Building and Old East, circa 1902. *University of North Carolina Library.*

the "Paris of the South," a place where artists and authors could go to be accepted and create.

With the lovely scenery and the free-spirited environment, Chapel Hill has always been a beacon of light. But even in the light, darkness can creep in. Along the tree-lined streets and brick buildings standing against the Carolina blue sky, there has been an evil that, from time to time, has bubbled up to the surface and brought the dreamers and scholars back to reality. However, every time evil visits, the story line seems to read, "These things never happen here." History has shown that it does happen here, time and time again.

Is it just a short memory that buries these events in the area's consciousness, or is there something else? Unsolved murders, conspiracies and questionable deaths by suicide mark the news over the years, but the stories just seem to fade away. While a few of these murders are well-known, most graduates of the university have never heard of most of the murders chronicled here. Most of the townspeople have never heard of many of the ghastly crimes that have become like bad dreams. Occasionally, you will find a local, the ever-elusive native North Carolinian who was born and raised in the area, who will remember some of these events. But their knowledge will generally end where their memory begins. After these murders pass through the memories of the townspeople, they seem to fade away.

But it is important to remember these things. History forgotten is history that will be repeated. Thinking that something bad will not happen to you because you go to an elite university or because you live in a gorgeous small town with a low crime rate can be dangerous. Evil cannot be denied, and the devil lurks everywhere—even in small-town America, where the veneer of safety can be broken like a thin piece of glass.

1

LEGEND OF A CRIME

It seems that from the very beginning of the university's time in Chapel Hill, there has been a dark cloud lingering between the majestic trees and the Carolina blue sky. Murder—or at least the rumor of murder—is intertwined with the story of Peter Dromgoole. Unlike later crimes, the line between fact and fiction becomes blurred in this case, but the dark undertone is there. If the stories are true, young Peter is the first victim on record in Chapel Hill, but he was not the last.

Peter Dromgoole was a wild and moody young man who spent just a short time in Chapel Hill, but the mark he left on the university and town is just as strong today and possibly stronger than it has ever been. He was born in Halifax County in 1815 to Edward Dromgoole the II and Sarah Pelham Dromgoole. His father was a merchant, physician and planter. His father had also been a Methodist minister who had emigrated from Ireland in 1770 after renouncing Catholicism, and he helped spread Methodism throughout North Carolina.

Edward was a hard man to please and had big hopes and even bigger expectations for his son Peter. Growing up on the Sligo Plantation near Roanoke Rapids, Peter received the finest education his parents could provide for him. Edward sent Peter out into the world in 1832 to Franklin Male Academy in Louisburg to finish his education and prepare himself to attend the state's premier university. He was there for only a year, and in 1833, he traveled across the state to apply to the University of Chapel Hill.

Edward Dromgoole was expecting great news from Peter, but his son's first letter from Chapel Hill did not give him comfort at all. Peter explained to his father in the letter that he had been rejected from the university by the admissions clerk but that he had hired a tutor and was studying really hard. He assured his father that he would be admitted into the university in June "with ease."

Filled with anger, Edward shot back a strongly worded letter to his son that started a back and forth between the two that came to a head when Edward also received a letter from one of the faculty members at UNC saying that Peter was squandering his time there. Edward knew his son well enough to know that he was most likely drinking and womanizing his way through Chapel Hill, as he had done this in Roanoke Rapids and Louisburg. His next letter was the harshest yet.

Peter did not take his father's scolding and wrote back, saying, "I have determined never to see that parent's face whom I have treated with so little respect." He concluded that he was sailing for Europe to make his own way. His father was fuming over his lack of commitment and doubted that the threat was real from Peter, but soon after receiving the letter, he was informed by the university that Peter had disappeared.

Peter's uncle George Dromgoole, a congressman from Virginia, went to Chapel Hill to find his nephew but found few clues about where he could have gone. Peter had left most of his possessions in his room and had told varying stories about his intentions. Some of the students said that he had indeed sailed for Europe, while others said that he had joined the army and headed out west. George never found out for sure where Peter went, but he did find out that Peter was considered "moody and wild" by everyone who knew him.

No one ever saw him or heard from him again. But his disappearance sparked rumors and legends that persist to this day. The most prominent of these is that Peter was enamored with a young woman named Fannie and had been spending most of his time wooing her instead of working toward gaining admittance to UNC. She was receptive to his attention, and they would picnic in an area known as Piney Prospect near the school. One day, another male student insulted the honor of Fannie, and Peter, who was no doubt already in a foul mood due to the letter from his father, challenged the young man to a duel.

Dueling was outlawed, but it was not an uncommon way to settle matters of honor in North Carolina at the time. The men met early one morning and stood back to back with their pistols in hand. They took their paces, turned and fired. Peter fell, and the other boys who had been a part of the

Gimghoul Castle sits secluded among the trees near the University of North Carolina's campus. *University of North Carolina Library.*

duel suddenly realized the finality of what they had been a part of. They huddled together and decided that they had to get rid of Peter's body as soon as possible to avoid prosecution. They took his body to the area where he had once spent so many happy hours with his lover, Fannie, and buried him along the rocks.

There is no way to know if this rumor is true, but it is probably the result of the overactive imaginations of college students. Most believe that the legend grew from the real-life events of 1837, in which Peter's uncle George participated in a duel in Northampton County and killed a man. Also, the later formation of a secret society named the Order of Gimghoul in 1889, which was originally named the Order of Dromgoole, perpetuated the rumors. The secret society is made up of prominent juniors, seniors and faculty members of UNC who are invited by current members. It is an Arthurian society based on chivalry and the traditions from the days of knights in shining armor. Furthermore, the construction of a Gothic castle–type house near Piney Prospect, where the society meets, has led to the spreading of the rumor and legend. Originally built in 1924 and named Hippol Castle—later changed to Gimghoul—the stone building stands alone among the foliage of Chapel Hill and serves as a landmark that keeps the legend alive.

Although Peter was never found or heard from again, it can be assumed that something happened to the young man that kept him from reemerging in North Carolina. He had been a child of privilege and ease. Even if he went on a journey to Europe or joined the army, if he survived, he would have shown back up after his adventure to take his place in his family. Most think that Peter either went to Europe or out west, met with some unfortunate accident and died as a nameless wanderer, unable to get home.

2

A SEASON OF TERROR

The months between the summers of 1877 and 1878 were terrifying in the village of Chapel Hill, North Carolina. The homes of ladies who were attending the North Carolina Normal School, where future teachers were being trained, were being targeted. Night after night, homes were entered and robbed, whether there were people home or the houses were empty. Ladies were assaulted, many items were stolen and the village was gripped with fear for months.

At the beginning of the reign of terror, the burglars showed a high level of boldness. In the late summer of 1878, a woman was awakened by the sound of movement inside her room. She had heard tell of burglaries recently and peered over her covers into the darkness with fear.

"Who's there?" she asked the darkness.

No one answered. She listened intently, but the room was silent. She tossed the covers back and stood up with the intention of lighting a candle. She wanted to assure herself that she was indeed alone in her home, but upon standing up, she was grabbed by a stranger from the darkness. She fought him as best as she could, but the man who had broken into her home was too strong for her. She momentarily broke away from the man and grabbed a hatchet that she had by her bed. The man who had once been the aggressor fled through her window and into the yard. Shaken, the woman called out for help, and her story hit the newspaper the next day. The uncomfortable feeling of being robbed now turned into a shared fright that drove the men of the village into the streets at night, patrolling for anything out of the ordinary or any strangers who were prowling around in the night.

Despite their best efforts, the burglaries continued. The most violent attack took place at the house of Mrs. Herndon in June 1878. Mrs. Herndon was awakened by the sound of someone talking and walking around her backyard. She roused herself from her bed and looked out the window into the darkness of the yard. It was still and quiet, and she wondered if she was just jumpy. Still, she felt more comfortable taking some precaution, so she grabbed a chair from the small writing desk in the corner and dragged it loudly across the room. Then she lit the lamp by her bed and shortened the wick so there would be some light in her room. She hoped that if someone was lurking about, they would know someone was awake in the house and move on. She climbed back into bed and closed her eyes.

Moments later, her worst nightmares came true when she suddenly heard the front door of the house being ripped from its hinges and heavy footsteps coming through the house, straight for her room. Mrs. Herndon sprang from her bed and ran across the room to the window. She heard her bedroom door burst open behind her, and she tried to pry the window open to scream for help. She managed to create a small opening when her attacker grabbed her, spun her around and struck at her with a hatchet. She parried the blow away with her arms as she fought for her life. All the while, she was screaming for her neighbor Dr. Mallett through the window.

"Doctor, Doctor, someone is killing me!" she screamed through the open window as she flung herself backward, trying to avoid the blows from her attacker. In the mostly dark room, she could see just a blur as the figure raised the hatchet above his head over and over to strike her.

While Mrs. Herndon fought for her life, Dr. Mallett heard her cries and, along with his son John, sprang into action. The men ran down the stairs of their house and out into the night. In the Herndon house, Mrs. Herndon's young daughter, not knowing how to respond, cowered in her room under the covers as she heard the screams from the attack. Two young Black men, Jim and Simon, who worked for Mrs. Herndon, were sleeping in the kitchen when they also heard her cries and ran into the house.

"The doctor is coming!" yelled Mrs. Mallett from her second-story window.

Mrs. Herndon's attacker heard the commotion and raised the hatchet once again for a death blow. He brought the weapon down and struck her head. Luckily, it was a glancing blow that sliced her head open and cut a piece of wood out of the windowsill. Mrs. Herndon fell back against the wall, limp and badly wounded. The assailant turned to run and heard footfalls on the stairs. Mrs. Herndon's daughter heard the footsteps and knew help was coming.

The home of Dr. Mallett. *North Carolina Archives.*

"The boys are coming!" she yelled from her room, knowing that Jim and Simon had arrived.

The attacker ran through the door and straight through the two young men as they came up the stairs, pushing them down as he went. He ran out of the front door and disappeared into the night.

Jim and Simon composed themselves as John and Dr. Mallett came into the house. They continued up the stairs together and found Mrs. Herndon lying in a pool of blood on the floor.

"Run back home and get my bag!" Dr. Mallett told John.

John hustled back down the stairs and across the yard to his house. He grabbed the black leather medical bag his father kept by the door and bolted back across the yard. He was surprised as he ran toward the house to see Alphonso Davis walking toward him in the dim light from the streetlamp. He slowed his gait as he approached him.

"What you doing out this time of night in your shirtsleeves John?" Alphonso asked.

"There has been another burglary," John said. "Mrs. Herndon is hurt bad!"

"I was just down at Griffins," he said as they passed. John knew who Davis was, but at the time, he was focused on the injured Mrs. Herndon and getting his father the tools he needed to help her. Davis seemed so cool and calm, it never struck John that he may have been involved.

Dr. Mallett was able to stitch up Mrs. Herndon, and the constables arrived at the house. They immediately arrested Jim and Simon, and it took the collective influence of the people on scene to convince them that the boys were not the responsible parties and were there to help. Jim and Simon were released, but precious time for canvasing the area and finding the real attacker had been lost. When the sun came up, a bloody hatchet was found in the grass of the Herndons' front yard. The village of Chapel Hill was now fully on alert. A reward of $500 was offered up for the capture of the burglars, and a detective was brought in from Richmond, Virginia. The burglaries in town slowed, but the break-ins outside of town increased. It seemed that this year of terror would not stop.

Dr. Mallett. *North Carolina Archives.*

The end came sooner than everyone thought. Reverend G.W. Purefoy lived two miles outside of Chapel Hill. One night, he was away from home, leaving his wife alone. Like so many times before, she heard sounds in the house in the dead of night. Lighting a candle, she found herself face to face with a man. Luck was on her side, as this man was not in possession of a hatchet and a murderous spirit like the man who had attacked Mrs. Herndon, and he turned and fled from her. She was shaken, but she was also able to identify the man she saw in her house. The law soon descended on Albert Atwater.

Atwater, a Black man, was known to the law in town, but he was not a suspect at the time of the burglaries. No one looked at him as someone who could be a part of so many heinous crimes. Atwater at first refused to talk to the police. They felt that he could not have acted alone, and he did not fit the description of the other burglar, who had been identified as a white man. The police tried to get information from Atwater, but he refused to talk. They pressured him to implicate his confederates, but he would not.

But Atwater began to see that he was going to be charged with everything and bear the burden of the crimes. When he was finally offered a deal for a lesser sentence, he suddenly found the motivation he needed to tell his tale.

What Atwater told the police was astounding. There had, in fact, been a gang of burglars. Their organizer and leader was Alphonso Davis, a white man who had been born and raised in Chapel Hill before heading out west in his young adult years to see if he could make his fortune. Davis came back to North Carolina and worked as a clerk at the Boyden House in Salisbury and then at the Yarbourough House in Raleigh. He came back to Chapel Hill after he was discharged from both employers and, some say, run out of town by the angry family members of young ladies whom he had dishonored. Back in Chapel Hill, he settled into a life of insolence, drunkenness and violence. He was a small-time crook with big plans.

Davis soon reached out to one of his friends, another white man named Henry Andrews, who was also born and raised in Chapel Hill. Andrews was also prone to idleness and petty crime. He was once accused of violating a woman in the town, but due to the reputation and questionable character of the woman, he was let go. Davis saw him as his lieutenant in a gang of highwaymen who would rob the better-off residents of the village and anyone who traveled through. They planned a crime spree the likes of which had never been seen in the piedmont area of North Carolina. However, as Alphonso Davis paced back and forth at one such planning session, he realized their group was too small. They needed more men.

Louis Carlton was a Black man who was also from Chapel Hill. He was a person, like Davis and Andrews, of low character. He was behind on his home payments and looking for easy money. Carlton was an easy recruit and reached out to the son-in-law of his mistress, Albert Atwater, who was also behind on his house payments and in need of money. Once Atwater was on board, the gang was off and running, as Atwater would later testify. His testimony of the gang's violent crimes was mostly verified by the testimony of others who were able to paint the complete picture of the group's actions.

Davis, Andrews and Carlton were arrested and later tried for the robbery of Mrs. Herndon. With the testimony of Atwater and John Mallett, the jury found the men guilty. The judge gave them no mercy and sentenced them to hang. When the verdict was read, Davis shouted that the witnesses had lied, Carlton sat silently and stared straight ahead and Andrews fainted. Atwater's life was spared for his testimony.

A crowd of ten thousand came to watch the men hang. A minister waited for them on the gallows as the men came up the wooden steps. He spoke quietly to each of them, and they took their positions, the executioner placing a rope around their necks. Davis and Andrews remained quiet and stoic throughout the process. The sheriff read a statement the men had written that professed their innocence and expressed their hope for salvation. Carlton spoke for fifty minutes, denying his involvement in the crimes and saying that he was going straight to Jesus upon the dropping of the trapdoor. When Carlton was finished, a hymn was sung, and a prayer was said for the men by the minister. The prisoners awkwardly shook hands with each other, despite their tied wrists. A silence fell over the crowd, and it was only broken by the dropping of the men and the jerking of the ropes. But death would not come quickly. Andrews dangled and struggled for thirteen minutes before his body fell limp. Davis's and Carlton's ropes were too long, and their toes touched the ground. Men had to pull the ropes back to shorten them; it took Carlton fourteen minutes to die and Davis fifteen.

The deaths of the men gave the townspeople comfort, as they knew that the stalkers who had terrorized them for over a year would strike no more. Carlton went to his grave leaving much speculation that he had also murdered his wife. Shortly after the crime spree had begun, his wife died suddenly and unexpectedly. Days after her death, Carlton married Albert Atwater's mother-in-law. A postmortem examination was done on his first wife, and it was found that she had ground glass and poison in her stomach. Carlton would not answer for her death on Earth, but he certainly did in eternity.

Albert Atwater left Chapel Hill for Greensboro, where he changed his name to John Taylor. He was soon in trouble, which culminated in his arrest for the rape of an elderly woman in Reidsville. While sitting in jail in Greensboro, a group of hooded men formed in the dead of night and marched to the jail. They demanded that Atwater be released to them, and he was. Atwater was brought outside of town and set on his own gray horse with a rope tied round his neck and thrown over an oak tree branch. The men stood staring at the frightened Atwater as he looked all around him at the hooded figures and their torches. Soon, a hand slapped the hindquarters of the horse, and the rope snapped tight. Carlton's body hung there all the next day. With his death, the gang of Chapel Hill burglars was gone.

3

LOVE TRIANGLE

Becky Lyon walked into the Hillsborough Courthouse on October 3, 1879. She was there to answer for the murder of Nannie Blackwell, her son Milton and her unborn child. With a solemn look on her face, she stared at the floor as her lawyers stood before the judge and jury on her behalf. She was there based on the accusations of Robert Boswell, who had already been convicted of the murders and was only alive to testify against the woman who he claimed had pushed him and helped him commit the murders. Gallows Hill awaited him no matter what the outcome of the trial was.

Becky was being represented by two of the premier lawyers in the state of North Carolina, Colonel Thomas Ruffin Jr. and John W. Graham. Ruffin was the son of North Carolina Supreme Court justice Thomas Ruffin Sr. Ruffin Jr. was a practicing lawyer in April 1861, when the Civil War erupted. He joined the Confederate army as a private in Alamance County and rose to the rank of lieutenant colonel. He fought in the Battles of Second Manassas, South Mountain and Sharpsburg, where he was severely wounded. After he was wounded, he returned to law and teamed up with a former major in the Confederate army, Major Graham. They served as the highest-profile lawyers in the state and sought trials that grabbed the headlines.

The trial lasted all day, with the lawyers calling witness after witness to counter the claims Boswell made against Becky. At 7:00 p.m., they finally stopped for the day and began again the next morning promptly at 9:00 a.m., with Becky Lyon once again solemnly staring at the floor as the evidence was discussed. Her face did not betray her emotions. Ruffin stood for his final presentation and pointed out the one thing that had not been deliberated: the source of the accusation. Robert Boswell was a man who had committed disgusting and unimaginable crimes, yet the prosecution wanted a jury of good citizens to believe his word to send a woman to her death. The jury deliberated and brought back its verdict. Becky stood, looking at the floor of the Orange County Courthouse with a straight face, hiding the fear and trepidation that coursed through her body. "Not guilty," came the verdict. A slight smile spread across Becky's face as she finally looked up and around the room.

Bob Boswell's body shook as he sat on his casket a few weeks later. The wagon cut through a crowd of three thousand spectators. Armed guards walked beside the wagon and pushed people aside as it made its way through town to Gallows Hill, which is today the corner of Nash and West Union Streets in Hillsborough. This was the same scaffold that had, the year before, been used to hang the Chapel Hill burglars Davis, Andrews and Carlton. But their crimes seemed to pale in comparison to the brutality of this man who moved toward his own demise. If hell had levels, the Chapel Hill burglars would face a lukewarm reception compared to the fiery pit that awaited Bob Boswell. When the wagon arrived at its final destination, the guards helped Boswell down, and he mounted the stairs to the platform. He looked out on the crowd who booed and jeered him. The chaplain Reverend Wheeler raised his hands, and the crowd was silenced. He read the confession Boswell had written before his journey into eternity and said a prayer, and the executioner placed the black hood of death over Boswell's head. The noose was next, and he pulled it down tight around Boswell's neck. At 1:25 p.m., the trapdoor was sprung, and Boswell's body dropped five feet below the platform, twisting and struggling for air. Boswell struggled in vain for the last few moments of his life, trying to find some way to survive. Death came slowly. Thirty minutes elapsed before a doctor was able to declare him dead. The crowd looked on at the swinging corpse. His neck had not been broken by his initial fall, and his death came by strangulation. Some solace was given to those who wanted Boswell to suffer as he had made others suffer.

Boswell's brutal crime spree had begun as a love triangle—as many do. Boswell and his common-law wife, Nannie Blackwell, lived in eastern Orange County with their son. In the fall of 1878, he caught the attention of young Becky Lyon. Becky was sharp, shrewd and energetic—she also always got what she wanted. She had previously set her sights on Ned Lyon, who was married, but his wife died suddenly. He and Becky were married soon after. Suspicion was cast on the death of Lyon's wife, but there was no proof of any wrongdoing by Ned, and he and Becky moved on from the tragedy as man and wife. Soon, however, Becky was restless, and she took up with Bob in an affair. In his confession, Bob claimed that Becky told him she had poisoned Ned's wife and was willing to poison Ned himself to get him out of the way if Bob would do the same so they could be together.

According to Boswell, he soon after tried to poison Nannie, but she only got sick. At the same time, he received news that Ned had suddenly passed away. Becky Lyon had poured arsenic into his glass of milk, and he soon died. Boswell was apprehensive about killing his wife, so he gained employment on the farm of Jeff Fisher in Raleigh to get some distance from Becky. He stayed away through the summer but finally returned to his family. Nannie was glad to see him, and he spent a few days at home as her husband—the way things had been before. But it was not long before the siren's call was too much for Boswell, and he made his way the half mile through the woods to Becky Lyon's house.

They spent the evening together, and by that night, she had him back on board for their original plan. Standing on the porch of her cabin, she watched as he walked into the darkness with an axe he would use to carry out the deed.

When Boswell arrived at his house, he stood in the front yard under a tree, looking at it. Silent darkness engulfed the small house, and the wind blew the tall grass around him. He took a deep breath, walked onto the porch and pushed the door open.

"Nannie," he called into the dark house.

"Yes," he heard her reply sleepily.

"Can you come out here on the porch a minute?" He could hear her stirring from her bed, and then she appeared at the door in her nightdress, rubbing her eyes. "Is everything alright?" she asked. Her eyes were clear in an instant as Bob raised the axe and swung it down toward her head. She moved to the side, and the blade sliced through her shoulder. She fell backward and came to her feet like a cat before running for the back door. Into the field behind her cabin, Nannie ran screaming as Boswell ran behind her with the axe above his head, ready to strike. Nannie, despite the blood that was gushing from her wounded shoulder, was outpacing her attacker until her feet became tangled in pea vines and she tripped. She rolled over in time to see her husband standing over her, bringing the axe down on her head. The crushing blow split her skull in two, and her last scream of terror hung in the night air, unfinished.

Bob laid the axe down among the pea plants and grabbed his wife's body under her arms. He began to drag her body back toward the cabin. His mind raced with more problems. "What about the boy?" he asked himself. Maybe he was asleep and didn't see or hear anything. That would be for the best. If his aim was truer, Nannie would have died instantly on the front porch, and he could have buried her. He dragged Nannie's body back into the house and into their bedroom. He looked into their son's room, and he was still slumbering in the faint moonlight that was shining through the window. Bob Boswell closed the back door of the cabin and walked back out to the front yard. He came back in the front door carrying a torch and threw it against the wall where his son slept. He then retreated out the front door, closed it behind him and went back to Becky's house.

Neighbors saw the flames quickly and rushed to put the fire out. While they toiled to save Boswell's house and family, he was fleeing to Raleigh in the hopes of establishing an alibi. Inside the house, there was no mistaking what had happened. The neighbors found the body of the boy in his bed, dead from smoke inhalation. Then they found the body of Nannie, who had obviously encountered a much more violent fate. When the autopsy of her body was done, it was discovered that she was with child once again at the time of her death. Suspicion immediately turned to Bob Boswell, and he was arrested in Raleigh and brought back to Orange County. His confession led to the trial against Becky Lyon and was the only thing that saved his life for a time that summer while he waited for her trial.

With his confession, he remined alive for a time longer than he should have. The jury, reluctant to condemn any woman to death, took into account Bob Boswell's violent murder of his family and the changing nature of his story to grant Becky her freedom. They may have not wanted to see a woman hang on their account, but they would never forget that at the root of the issue was the affair between Becky and Bob Boswell and that six lives were lost at the end of that affair. Mostly, the jury would never forget the way Becky's solemn face broke into a sly smile as the foreman read the not guilty verdict.

4

THE MURDER OF DEPUTY SHERIFF D. JOSEPH NICHOLS

When Deputy Sheriff Joseph Nichols received a warrant on that warm September day in 1904, he couldn't help but feel a great deal of trepidation and nerves. An experienced deputy in Orange County, he had run-ins with the subject of the warrant before. He pinched the bridge of his nose and closed his eyes, then rubbed his forehead. He read it again. James Knapp Horner was wanted for beating his son's wife. Deputy Nichols knew Horner as well as everyone else in the county did and knew there would be trouble. Thoughts of his wife and four children ran through Deputy Nichols's head, as did the words of Horner himself the last time they had a run-in: "If you ever come for me again, I'll kill you." Nichols took out his revolver and disengaged the cylinder, rolling it in his fingers and making sure he had a round in each chamber. He closed it, checked the action, holstered his weapon and grabbed his hat on the way out the door.

Horner was a farmer and landowner in northern Orange County. He owned two farms, both over one hundred acres, and should have been a prominent and respected man in the community. He was prominent, though not in the way that would bring him into the fold of polite society. He was also a "blockader," or moonshiner, as most would refer to him now. He was known widely as a bad man who was violent and mean. Skinny, tall and with jet-black hair, Horner had a goatee and a look of evil in his eye, and most people tried as hard as they could to stay clear of him. He was part of a network of moonshiners in the backwoods of the county. He had been in trouble with the law many times before but always seemed to walk away without any consequences. The connections of the moonshiner network ran deep, and it frustrated the sheriff and his deputies.

When Deputy Nichols arrived at the Horner farm, Horner was gone. His wife said he was hunting. Nichols moved off into the woods, where he was told he could find Horner. Nichols was now more nervous than before. There was always a good chance that Horner was armed, but there would be no doubt now. Deputy Nichols was aware that he was moving toward danger, and he could hear his heartbeat as he moved through the woods, calling out for Horner. Soon, Nichols found Horner leaning against a tree with his shotgun draped over his arm and a scowl across his face. Horner knew why Deputy Nichols was there and also knew that he had ruined any hopes he had of hunting by stomping and yelling through the woods like a damn fool. Nichols was aware that Horner was mean and that he was a Confederate veteran of the Civil War. Horner had also been acquitted of killing a man before on the grounds of self-defense. Deputy Nichols remembered the threat Horner had made and imagined that if he were to go through with it, it would not be his first time killing a man.

A tense moment and a few threats and curses between the two led to a flash of violence. Nichols put his hand on his pistol and demanded that Horner come with him. Horner was not to be moved, and he snapped the barrel of his shotgun closed and raised it toward Nichols in an instant. The deputy pulled his revolver, but before he could fire, Horner emptied both barrels into the deputy. The buckshot tore open the left side of Nichols, and he fell to the ground. Nichols harmlessly fired a round from his revolver into the air. Horner walked over to him as he reloaded his gun. He stood over the dying man and kicked the pistol away from him, then walked away back toward his house.

The shots had aroused some men in the woods, and they found Nichols. They tried to get him out of the woods and to a doctor, but he died within the hour. An enraged group of men swarmed the sheriff's office as they learned of the killing. They were tired of Horner and the blockaders of Orange County. More than forty men set off to bring Horner to justice. When they reached his house, they found that he had slipped away into the woods, so they followed. The search brought about no results, but then before sundown, Horner appeared out of the woods and started moving across a cornfield. He was surrounded by the posse, who demanded he stop and give himself up. He appeared unarmed but cursed the men and said he was going home and would not be taken by them. The men began to fire on him with "bird shot," shotgun rounds with small pellets. Horner was struck several times in the side and finally in the face. He was taken into custody with wounds that were not life-threatening and taken to jail.

During Horner's first night in jail, the sheriff had a problem on his hands. As he looked out of the window, he could see men gathering around the jailhouse. He feared a lynching would occur, as deputy Nichols was a beloved man. The sheriff sent two deputies to guard Horner as he traveled by train to Durham, where he would be turned over to the Durham County sheriff. When Horner settled into the Durham jail, reporters came to see him. Swollen and bloodied, he held court with the journalists.

"I guess they will hang me, but they cannot keep me out of many years. I am now fifty-eight years of age and would not have lived more than ten years longer. I will lose my corn crop though on account of being arrested." He then became somewhat reflective. "I ought not to have killed him, I guess. But he shot at me, and I had to fire at him. I did not intend to kill him." This was the argument Horner would use in his trial, as he claimed he killed the deputy in self-defense. Having the resources to hire defense attorneys, Horner made a good run at gaining his freedom. He argued that Nichols had pulled out his pistol and shot at him first and that he was just defending himself. It was a defense based solely on his word, since Nichols did not live to tell his side of the story. His version of the shootout was whispered through dying lips. In 1905, Horner was convicted of second-degree murder and sentenced to twelve years of hard labor, which, to a fifty-nine-year-old man, was a death sentence. To this day, Deputy Joseph Nichols is the only Orange County deputy to lose his life in the line of duty, and may he remain so by the grace of God.

5

THE EFLAND BANK ROBBERY

On November 1, 1930, at 10:30 a.m., a yellow Buick pulled up in front of the Efland Bank. A small man got out of the car and entered the bank while another sat behind the wheel, looking around. Mrs. Shambley crossed the street from Forrest's Store to make a deposit at the bank. As she approached the bank door, the man in the car spoke to her.

"Lady, you can't go in there."

"Excuse me?" she said, stopping to look at the man who was looking back at her in the side mirror of the car.

"You can't go in the bank. We're attending to business in there right now."

His eyes were penetrating, and his voice conveyed more than the words he said. She knew there was trouble in the bank, and she turned and retreated across the street.

Inside, bank president J.L. Efland and cashier Robert Riley were working on preparing the payroll for the Efland Hosiery Mill when they heard the door open. Despite having been robbed just a few weeks earlier, they figured this was one of the regular folks who came in the bank. A small town like Efland didn't have strangers usually. This day, however, they were mistaken, as a small man holding a gun appeared in the open doorway that separated the lobby from the office area.

"Throw 'em up," the small man ordered as he brandished a revolver at the two men. They put their hands up and stepped back away from the money. The small man moved across the room and pushed the two men into a corner. He then began to grab cash by the handful and throw it into a canvas sack as he watched the two men. When he got through the money on the counter, he opened the drawers and took the money from them. Robert Riley saw an opening as the robber looked into the drawers, and he started to crowd him.

"Get back," the robber yelled as he raised the pistol into Riley's face. Riley retreated to the corner with Efland and watched as the man made his final inspection of the drawer.

Mrs. Shambley walked back into Forrest's Store, where Carl Forrest was still behind the counter.

"Is everything OK?" he asked, seeing the distressed look on her face.

"Something is wrong over at the bank," she said, pointing through the window at the yellow Buick with the stranger behind the wheel. Mr. Forrest took his double-barrel shotgun from behind the counter and walked out to the street.

"Get back inside!" the man in the Buick cried.

Mr. Forrest took a step back onto the porch of his store as he heard the man blowing the car's horn.

Inside, the robber, hearing the signal, finished his work and began to back out of the bank. As he backed up, Robert Riley stepped forward. He had been robbed before and was not so intimidated by the bank robber.

"Yeah, you identified the fella that came in here before. I want to tell you now that if you identify me, I'll get you. If I don't, I have a buddy that will. Understand? And if you poke your head out of this door in ten minutes after I'm gone, you will be a goner. I've a buddy planted out there."

Riley looked at him with disgust as he reached the front door.

"That applies to both of you!" said the robber as he looked over at Efland and disappeared from view into the street.

Carl Forrest saw the robber step out of the bank, and their eyes met. The robber with the pistol hesitated for a moment, raised the revolver and fired two shots at him. After he fired, the robber turned back toward the Buick and ran. Forrest was jolted into action by the shots, which whizzed by his head and thudded into the front of his store. He raised his shotgun and pulled the trigger. The small man fell forward, sliding in the dirt with a great wound in the center of his back. The Buick backed up, and the man tried to stand as his accomplice threw open the door and reached for him. Another shot rang out, and the small man fell dead. The getaway driver slammed the door of the Buick and drove off as other men appeared on the scene, firing a variety of pistols, shotguns and rifles after him.

Robert Riley appeared on the street, and he and Carl Forrest walked over to the dead man and peered down at his body. A search though his jacket told them that his name was Bruce Carpenter of Durham. Efland was a small town with no law enforcement, so the Orange County sheriff was called in. Carpenter was an orphan who had been in trouble with the law most of his life. He had recently been released from the North Carolina State Hospital for the Insane. He was only twenty-three years old, and his life of crime had led him to his death there in the dirty street of Efland in front of the bank. A canvas bag with $1,800 was still clutched in his hand as law enforcement picked up his body and carried it away to be buried.

The driver of the car was soon identified as Winifred Riley, no relation to Robert Riley. He was another Durham resident, and the Durham County sheriff soon had his men on the lookout for him. Within a few days, the yellow Buick was found, and it was determined it had been stolen in Charlotte. Winifred Riley was arrested in Durham and sent back to Orange County for trial. It didn't take long for the jury to sentence him to seven to ten years in prison for his part in the robbery. But that was not the end of the story.

A few weeks after the robbery, while Winifred Riley sat in jail waiting for his trial, a bank examiner walked into the Efland Bank and showed his identification to Robert Riley. He told him he was there to audit the bank since it had been robbed. Riley stood up from his desk and took his keys out of his pocket.

"You don't need to make a check," he said. "I'm done."

Surprised, the auditor asked Riley what he meant. Riley picked up the ledger book from his desk and handed it to the auditor. "You are a good bookkeeper," he said. "It is all right here." Robert Riley walked out of the bank as the auditor and T.J. Efland looked at each other in shock. They soon figured out what Riley was talking about. Checking the books, the auditor found that the bank was about $40,000 short. Robert Riley was questioned and arrested and ended up a few cells down from Winifred Riley in the Orange County Jail.

Robert would not say where the money was at first. He just said over and over that he had not spent a penny of it or profited from the shortage at all. He was well known and loved in town. His wife said she had no idea what had happened to the money, as they existed, much like their neighbors, in poverty. Finally, it was determined that Riley had been making loans to his neighbors and local farmers who had no money to pay their bills or feed their families. The Great Depression had hit the county hard, and Riley could not refuse to give aid to those most in need, whether they could pay the bank back or couldn't. Despite his good intentions, Riley found himself sentenced, just like Winifred Riley to seven to ten years in prison for a much different crime—but a crime, nonetheless. The bank never recovered and soon folded, leaving the people of Efland without its financial services. The robbers had been unsuccessful in getting away with the $1,800, but they had been successful in exposing what was a far greater shortage at the bank.

6

THE UNIVERSITY HOT DOG STAND ROBBERY

On January 20, 1920, the Volstead Act was enacted, and the era of Prohibition began in the United States. Over the next thirteen years, crime boomed in the country as people flocked to illegal distributors to wet their whistles. Chapel Hill, being a college town, was no different, and its citizens found solace in underground drinking establishments all over town. From the back of the Esso station that soon would become the famous Brady's Restaurant to a shack near where the Blue Cross Blue Shield building stands today, residents and travelers drank their fill, even though it was a crime. Black residents of the town frequented the Blind Tiger, a speakeasy located where the Village Apartments stand today.

Chapel Hill did not turn into another southern Chicago, with gangs fighting for territory and federal officers raiding speakeasys like the movies portray. The fight against illegal alcohol in North Carolina was much more subtle. The Chapel Hill police chief was rumored to have told his officers every year when the new crop of students arrived at the university to arrest the first kid they saw walking crooked and make an example of them. After that, as long as alcohol was not flaunted in the public, it would be ignored for the most part. Even so, it seems that one instance of crime can be attributed to a dispute between those people who were working outside the law to bring booze to Chapel Hill.

Shortly after 9:00 p.m. on Thursday, March 31, 1932, four men in a Hudson pulled up to the University Hot Dog Stand on Franklin Street. Two men got out, and the other two men in the car pulled around and parked by the fire station on Columbia Avenue. The two men who had exited the Hudson entered the restaurant, sat at the counter and ordered sandwiches, pie and a couple of Dr Peppers. The clerk took their order on his notepad, then hustled back to the cook to get the food going. He couldn't help but notice how the two men eyed the owner of the hot dog stand, George Coleman, as he walked around the restaurant, talking to customers and bussing tables. Coleman was a businessman, and he was thought to have "investments" around town in the booze trade.

The clerk brought the men their Dr Peppers, and they each took a sip, never taking their eyes off Coleman. Suddenly, the two men stood up and walked around the counter, through the kitchen and out the back door. The cook watched them walk by as the grease popped on the flattop grill, and the clerk who took their order called out to Coleman, who looked up from the conversation he was having with a customer and excused himself. He followed the two men out the door and found them looking at an old icebox that had been dragged out behind the restaurant after it broke down months before.

"How much do you want for this old icebox?" one of the men asked. Confused and caught off guard, George Coleman rubbed his chin and looked at the icebox. Mud from the ground had been spattered on the sides of the icebox, and grass had grown around it. "Why would they want to buy this old thing?" he thought.

Suddenly, the other man brought a stick out from behind his back and struck Coleman over the head. He fell down but rolled back over to a crouching position to face his attackers. George Coleman was badly wounded and bleeding, but he was no pushover. The men approached him, and he hurled himself toward one of his attackers. They fought, and Coleman ended up on top of him, pummeling him with his fists, while the other man tried to pry him off of his partner. Soon, however, the blood from the wound on Coleman's head began to run into eyes, and he had to stop his attack. He was pulled off the man he was fighting and staggered around the building to Franklin Street, yelling for help at the top of his lungs. The driver of the Hudson gunned the engine and picked up the two men as they ran out from behind the hot dog stand. They sped off toward Carrboro.

Passersby called out for the police, and Officer U.M. Rackley emerged from the Carolina Theatre just as the Hudson sped past him. The citizens pointed as the men fled, and Rackley ran to the nearest car he could find. Sitting in front of the restaurant was a brand-new Cadillac. Behind the wheel was twenty-two-year-old Ashby Penn, the son of American Tobacco

Company vice-president Charles E. Penn. Handsome, charming and rich, the UNC junior was the model of American manhood at the time. Sitting beside him was his new fiancée, Ann Edmunds. They were enjoying a night out when they saw the commotion happening. When Rackley approached them to commandeer the car, Penn was more than willing to oblige. Rackley jumped on the running board, and Penn pulled out to follow the Hudson. Another local man, Robert Stone, jumped onto the other side of the car, and they were off.

The men sped down Graham Road, their car's headlights cutting through the darkness, when suddenly, one of the Cadillac's tires burst, sending the car swerving. Penn slowed the vehicle but noticed that just ahead of them was a car stopped in the road. The Cadillac slowed, and the men could see it was the Hudson. The Cadillac pulled up behind the car with its headlights shining directly on it. Rackley hopped off the car's running boards, and Penn exited the car. What happened next was disputed by both parties, but somehow, Penn ended up with Rackley's pistol and advanced on the car with Rackley following behind him with a flashlight. Stone later testified that Rackley gave the pistol to Penn, while Rackley said that Penn had just taken it.

The men approached the car with Penn in the lead, and as he reached the door of the car, he flung it open. It seems that shots were fired simultaneously by one of the men in the car and Penn. The man in the car was shot in the arm, and Penn was shot in the chest. Penn staggered back and fell into the ditch. Rackley ducked through the light coming from the car's headlights and ran into the darkness. Stone dipped behind the Cadillac, and Edmunds lowered herself down in the car. Men suddenly poured out of the Hudson. The three men who were not wounded bolted into the night. Stone ran over to Penn and dragged him back to the car. He lifted him into the backseat, and Ann Edmunds, who had taken the wheel, drove past the Hudson and up the road about a mile, where they stopped and took a look at Penn.

Penn was hurt badly, and the men knew he needed help soon or he would not make it. Stone ran up the road to look for help or another car that could take them to the hospital. Edmunds watched him run off into the darkness, but she soon decided she could not wait for him. She turned the car around and began to head back to Chapel Hill on three tires. She passed the Hudson, which was heading in the opposite direction, away from town. The wounded man had gotten the stalled car to start again, and he was driving with a bullet hole in his arm. Along the way, Edmunds, Stone and Penn came across Officer Rackley, who was walking along the road toward the town. When they reached Chapel Hill, they took Penn to the infirmary, where they gave him first aid and sent him along to Duke Hospital.

In the aftermath of the incident, Robert Stone found his way to a farmhouse, where they offered him help, but by the time he got back to the scene, everyone was gone. His testimony would be invaluable to the police in the later investigation. They immediately did not believe that robbery was a motive due to the ties Coleman had to bootleggers and the fact that the Hudson was a known vehicle used to run liquor. While Penn languished in Duke Hospital, teetering on the edge of death, the police went to work. Sheriff W.T. Sloan followed up on the fact that he knew one of the men had been shot by Penn, and he was able to track down Elwood Johnson, who soon identified the three other men who were in the Hudson. Lawrence Armstrong, Jack Thomas and Robert Thomas, who had once served as the chief of police for the small town of Mount Holly, were the others involved. The men were soon rounded up and tried.

Luckily for them, Penn survived his gunshot wound, and they avoided a murder charge. Johnson, Armstrong and Robert Thomas were sentenced to eight months in prison for their part in the "robbery" and attack of George Coleman. Jack Thomas, who was identified as the shooter of Ashby Penn, was sentenced to four years on a road crew, but he was later released after two years. Officer Rackley was soon dismissed from the police department due to the loss of confidence from the people of the town.

Ashby Penn recovered and married Ann Edmunds. They moved to Syracuse, New York, and began to raise a family together. Penn died in 1950 while he was the district manager of the Eastern Coal Sales Corporation. Although he was only thirty-nine years old at the time of his death, he had lived a full and eventful life. After graduating from college, he became a businessman and left a very successful career to become a patrol boat commander in the United States Navy during World War II. Ann had known Penn was a hero long before his service in the South Pacific and made sure she kept his memory alive for his son and daughter. She retold the story of the great hot dog stand robbery of 1932 to them over and over for the rest of her life.

7

GUNNED DOWN

Helen Massey was a good girl. Everyone who knew the seventeen-year-old young woman thought so. She was a quiet, well-mannered, smart and well-behaved churchgoing girl who always did her best in school. She was a girl with a bright future ahead of her, and her parents gushed over her whenever they had the chance. It seemed like she had it all, but she had one flaw: bad judgment. By the time May 6, 1935, rolled around, she had been on a rollercoaster of emotions over a man.

Twenty-three-year-old George Alston was not as well thought of as Helen. He worked as a butler and gardener for English professor Dr. Roland McClamrock. Dr. McClamrock was satisfied with his work as a butler, but Helen's mother spotted the bad apple from a mile away, and as soon as she found out about the love affair between Alston and her daughter, she sat Helen down and let her know how things were going to be. She told Helen that Alston was older than her and had only one thing on his mind. Helen's mother said he was a lazy and undesirable mate for her daughter. Helen was resistant at first, but soon she saw the tell-tale signs her mother warned her about, and she broke things off with him. He did not take this well.

Alston stole the McClamrocks' family car but brought it back after it was reported stolen by Dr. McClamrock. When Alston brought the car back, McClamrock was surprised by this action and was willing to keep him on and give him another chance. What McClamrock did not notice was that his .45-caliber army revolver was also missing. Alston had taken it and set off to see how drunk he could get before looking for Helen. He found her a little

The Varsity Theater. *From the* Yackety Yak.

after 10:30 p.m. as she was coming out of the Carolina Theater on Franklin Street with a friend. Helen saw him coming, and the smile ran away from her face as she turned to walk the other way. He called after her, but she wanted nothing to do with rehashing the breakup. Helen just wanted to avoid the confrontation and the argument. They had gone through it all repeatedly. Helen let Alston know things would just not work out between their age difference and the fact that her mother was so wholeheartedly against the relationship. Although Helen had a lapse in her better judgment, once she came to the end, she was done. But as Helen walked away from him, she turned just for a moment to try to convey her insistence on their separation and noticed that in his hand by his side, he held a pistol.

Terror ran through Helen, and adrenaline pumped through her body, pushing her flight instincts into overdrive. She bolted across the street to Ruth Durham's Restaurant, Alston hot on her heels. She burst through the doors, where she yelled, "George Alston is after me and has a gun!" Ernest Booth, who worked at the restaurant, saw the fear in her eyes and saw the man who was coming across the street with a revolver. He ran to the door and locked it. He grabbed her by the arm and pulled her toward the back door. Behind them, they could hear George Alston beating and kicking the door. As they reached the back door, the thudding blows to the front door stopped. The pair stood in silence for a moment. They looked back at the front door, and he was gone.

"He is going around back," Booth said as he led her back to the front door. He put his hand on the lock and looked back at her. "When I open the door, you run as fast as you can," he said.

He flipped the latch and turned the knob to open the door, and suddenly, it burst open. Her stalker had not gone around the building; instead, he had hidden himself with his ear to the door, waiting for it to open. When he heard the lock turn, he stepped in front of the door and gave it a kick. Booth was flung to the floor, and Helen screamed in horror as Alston stepped into the restaurant, pointing the pistol at her. He shot four times, hitting her in the face and the back as her body spun around. Two of his shots missed, and he was back out the door as fast as lightning. Booth regained his feet in time to see Alston run to his stolen car and speed off. A crowd had begun to gather, and Booth went to the mortally wounded girl who was dying on the floor of the lonely restaurant. As he knelt by her, she died—a beautiful girl with a bright future gone like a flame that had been blown out.

George Alston was captured soon after he fled and was taken to Hillsborough, where he confessed to the crime. He said that if he could not have Helen, he would make sure no one else could. Justice came swiftly for George Alston. At his trial, Dr. McClamrock testified to the faithful service of Alston, as did other professors who had spent time at the McClamrocks' house. O.J. Coffin, the head of the journalism department, and Dr. R.H. Wettach testified as character witnesses and felt that it must have been the whiskey or temporary insanity that gripped Alston before the slaying. The defense also brought in Dr. Harry W. Crane, an expert on abnormal psychology, who testified that Alston had the mental capacity of a child. The prosecution countered this with testimony from witnesses of the crime, as well as the testimony of Dr. Ashby, the superintendent of the state hospital in Raleigh, who said that Alston was perfectly capable of determining what was right and wrong. He was found guilty.

By September 1936, Alston found himself standing on the precipice of eternity in the form of the State of North Carolina's electric chair. Without a governor's pardon, Alston found himself walking down the cold concrete hallway to the final judgment at Central Prison in Raleigh. On September 4, 1936, Alston's payment came due for taking the life of Helen Massey. Alston looked scared as he walked shirtless into the execution room and waved shyly at the small group of spectators who were present to see his death. As he was strapped to the chair, Alston looked up at the gray ceiling and began to pray. The priest said a prayer, and the executioner flipped the switch. The lights waned and flickered for two minutes and fifty seconds as electricity coursed through Alston's body. When the current was turned off and Alston's body fell limp in the chair; the doctor placed his stethoscope to his chest and listened intently. The doctor looked at the executioner and shook his head. There was still a faint heartbeat. The executioner once again flipped the switch for another minute and thirty-five seconds, which was enough to end George Alston's life.

The day before his death, Alston scrawled a note with pencil on a rough piece of paper, praising the support of the McClamrock family and asking God to bless them. The note ended with, "Boys and girls, I want to advise you all to be pertickler [*sic*] and watch your love affairs, for it will cause you to lose your happy life please take my advice from the dust we came to dust we return blessed be the name of the lord so I am gone to rest…goodbye to the world."

8

THE BODY IN EASTWOOD LAKE

On May 20, 1944, the attendant who was working at the garage used by customers of the Washington Duke Hotel in Durham, North Carolina, walked by a black Packard that had been sitting there for over a week. He was knocked back by the rancid odor coming from the vehicle and had to take a handkerchief from his pocket to get near the car. He could see what appeared to be bloodstains on the upholstery of the vehicle. He ran back to the garage's office and called the Durham Police Department. The responding officer, Captain W.E. Gates, saw the same thing the attendant had seen and tracked the owner of the car. Its owner was Addie Jewett, sixty-seven, of Booneville, Missouri. The car had been left by her grandson, who was a guest at the hotel in room 1201.

Gates called the department for help and proceeded to the room, where he found Mr. Martin, Mrs. Jewett's grandson, along with a friend and two soldiers. He was compelled by the officers to come with them back to the car. When Martin opened the trunk, the smell of rotten flesh came flooding out. The men all held their noses as Captain Gates peered into the trunk. He could see a hatchet partially wrapped in brown paper and maggots crawling all about, making it appear like the floor of the trunk was alive and moving on its own. He and the other officers looked at Martin, who stood back from the sight. They asked if he could explain this, and he claimed he had hit a buzzard on the drive from Missouri and had bought three chickens on the way, put them in the trunk and forgotten about them. The officers did not buy this story and took him downtown for further questioning.

Martin was questioned, and the police went back to his hotel room, where they found a bloodstained shirt and pair of pants. They also found a will that had recently been signed by Mrs. Jewett, leaving $500,000 to Martin and an equal amount to his mother, who lived in Charlotte. Upon further review of the car, a lady's watch, a pair of broken glasses and false teeth were found in the glove box. Both the teeth and the watch had pieces of decomposed flesh attached to them. In the ashtray were a set of house keys and a keychain with the address 221 North Bridge Street in Chapel Hill. When police arrived at the house, they were struck by the same odor that was present in the Cadillac.

In the house, many women's clothing items were found, including a coat, shoes and a dress. A pillow with the words "Hotel Frederick" was found lying on the floor. While searching the house, the police were tipped off to a boat that was found on the bank of the small Eastwood Lake nearby that had a foul odor emanating from it as well. The search immediately shifted to the water, and soon, the body of Addie Jewett was recovered from the depths. She had been killed by several incredible blows to the head, and her body showed signs of twenty to twenty-five stab wounds. Edward Martin was indicted for murder, and soon, through his attorney, he came out with a "confession" of sorts, explaining how the death of his grandmother had been an accident. His statement read as follows:

> *The death of my grandmother, Mrs. Addie M. Jewett, has weighed so heavily upon my mind and conscience that I feel I must make a statement as to what actually occurred.*
>
> *I had been my grandmother's constant companion ever since earliest childhood, having few other close friends. I started drinking somewhat during the last year of college. My grandmother was much opposed to liquor in any form.*
>
> *That afternoon in Booneville, I bought a bottle of rum, and before dinner on the evening of May 9, 1944, I drank a good deal of the rum. After dinner, which we had at Holt's Café, at about 8:30 p.m., we drove out to the country. While we were driving, my grandmother attempted to take the liquor away from me. I refused to give it to her and pushed her away from me because her efforts were interfering with my driving the car. She fell over against the door of the car and must have struck the handle of the door because the door flew open, and she fell out on the road.*
>
> *I did not intend to hurt her. I quickly put on the brakes, shoved the car into reverse gear and started backing up. In the haste and panic caused*

Eastwood Lake, where the body of Mrs. Addie Jewett was discovered. *Author's collection.*

by this, the car must have traveled backwards faster and farther than I realized. I think some under portion of the car struck her, and I believe the front wheel passed over some part of her body, too.

I immediately jumped out of the car and ran to her. She was bleeding badly, and I knew she was terribly hurt. I put her in the car after much difficulty and started to the hospital with her. She gasped two or three times and then stopped breathing. I knew she had died, and I was very shocked and upset.

I intended to take the body to the hospital and notify the police. The nearer I came to town, the more frightened and mentally confused I became. I drove by the hospital but was unable to bring myself to stop. I then drove around, intending to notify the police, but was unable to bring myself to do so.

I drove around for some time and made up my mind that I would take the body to my mother, who lives in Charlotte, and tell her what had happened. After convincing myself beyond doubt that my grandmother had passed away, I put her body in the back of the car in the trunk, placing her head upon pillows in as comfortable a position as possible.

On my way to Charlotte, sometimes I thought I had better dispose of the body in some secluded place. I crossed large rivers, through mountains

> *and woods, and by big lakes, all of which offered ample opportunity for disposal. However, I kept to my first resolution of taking the body to my mother in Charlotte. I drove up to my mother's home, but by that time, the body had become so decomposed that I could not bring myself to tell my mother. I then decided that the best thing to do was to leave Charlotte and try to dispose of the body. I finally left the body in Eastwood Lake and went back to Durham, where I was arrested. No one helped me in any way.*
>
> *All the events leading up to and including my grandmother's death occurred in Cooper County, Missouri, and I want to waive extradition, go back and take the consequences. This statement is made feely and without compulsion.*

Edwards felt he needed a home court advantage when he went to trial, but he was soon disappointed. He was indeed transferred back to Missouri for trial. His attorney claimed that he had suffered temporary insanity during the incident, but medical examiners deemed him sane. Next, many family members and friends of the family were brought in to testify about the life Martin had lived. They told the story of an overbearing grandmother who had meddled in her daughter's marriage until it ended when Edward was a small boy. She had insisted that she take over the rearing of the boy, and he had been with her ever since. Edward was forbidden from playing with other boys and when he went to school, he had five minutes to get home and then two hours of piano lessons a day. Wherever she went, he was expected to go. If she went and sat on the porch, he had to go sit on the porch. When she decided to go inside, he had to follow.

When Edward was old enough to go to college, he had to commute instead of moving into a dorm. He drove thirty miles a day to school until he transferred to Duke University in Durham, North Carolina, to study chemistry. Distance did not equate to freedom for Edward, as his grandmother moved with him to North Carolina while he studied there. The witnesses for the defense painted the picture of a lonely, friendless young man who had spent his life under the thumb of his grandmother.

Nevertheless, the prosecution was able to bring in the evidence found from the car and the rented house in Chapel Hill, as well as the brutally beaten and stabbed, weighed-down body of Addie Jewett that had been recovered from Eastwood Lake. Witnesses also testified that the two had last been seen together (the last time Mrs. Jewett was seen alive) at the Frederick Hotel in Missouri on May 8, 1944. Around midnight on May 9, hotel employee Jake Allen was summoned by Edward to the room and was asked to bring two

Edward Martin brutally murdered his grandmother for money. *Chapel Hill Newspapers.*

bags and a pillow for his grandmother's comfort. Before Edward left, he paid for the room for a month in advance.

Throughout the trial, Edward Martin maintained a solemn demeanor. He dressed in fine clothing and came in every day with his hair slicked back and shoes shined. At lunch recesses, he would change into a new shirt for the afternoon. The media tried to glean out of the odd man any information they could get. On the day the verdict was read, a reporter asked him if he would rather be sent to the mental hospital or to prison. "At the hospital, I would be chained up with the insane murderers, and if I go to prison, I will have to work. I don't want to work, and I won't work," he replied.

When the verdict came down, Edward was convicted to twenty years in prison for second-degree murder. He became prisoner 58375 and settled into his job as a clerk. He was for all intents and purposes a model prisoner after adjusting to his role. At first, he complained incessantly about the prison's food and living conditions, but he eventually calmed down. He briefly escaped in 1950, but after a shoot-out with a pair of men he was drinking with, he was recaptured and sent back to finish his sentence.

9

THE EXECUTION OF JOHN HENRY BREEZE

Lettie McDade walked through the brisk late winter air of a February morning. She was on her way to see her neighbor, Agnes Wilkerson, a seventy-one-year-old widow who lived in a small house in northern Orange County. She visited her often and looked forward to the company and small talk. Everything seemed normal, like any other visit, until Lettie reached the door of the small home. As she raised her hand to knock, the smell of smoke wafted over her. Lettie knocked on the door quickly and with force. "Agnes!" she called.

Sensing that something was awry, Lettie opened the door and stepped inside. A haze of white smoke hung across the ceiling of the living room, which appeared to be ransacked. "Agnes!" Lettie called again as she pushed deeper into the house to the bedroom of Mrs. Wilkerson; there, she stopped in the doorway and covered her mouth, taking in the scene that met her eyes. Lying in her bed was Mrs. Wilkerson, her face badly beaten and the bed smoldering around her. Lettie screamed and grabbed a towel off a chair and began to smother out the smoldering mattress; she then looked to her friend. Mrs. Wilkerson moaned in pain and frailly reached out her hand to her friend. Lettie helped Mrs. Wilkerson out of her bed and then ran out of the house to find help. Neighbors helped Agnes Wilkerson into the backseat of a car, and she was taken to the hospital in Burlington, where she was treated for her wounds and burns. Soon, Orange County sheriff S.T. Latta showed up at the hospital. Even in her critical state, Mrs. Wilkerson was a great witness. Her hands trembled as she told her story to the sheriff.

She said she had bought a bundle of firewood from John Henry Breeze, a man who lived close by and worked at the sawmill. John Breeze was a slight and frail man. He had limited use of his left arm and walked with a limp. At thirty-three years old, he was small, which made him seem less intimidating and more inviting for a woman like Mrs. Wilkerson, so she asked him for help and invited him into her home. Mrs. Wilkerson told the sheriff that he brought the wood into her house, and when she asked him to put some wood on the fire, he took a piece from the stack and then turned to walk toward her. She opened her mouth to ask him what he was doing, but before she could speak, he attacked her, viciously beating her in the head and face with the piece of firewood. As she lay semiconscious on the floor, he picked her up and carried her into her bedroom, where she watched helplessly as he tried to set fire to the bed.

Mrs. Wilkerson could hear him ransacking her house as she lay on the bed, feeling the heat from the fire as it crept toward her skin. She finally lost consciousness. Luckily, the bed did not catch fire completely and began to smolder before it caught up and burned her alive. Although Mrs. Wilkerson was slightly burned, she found herself mostly in danger from the wounds she sustained in the initial attack. Sheriff Latta set out to find Breeze, who was at his home. He admitted taking the wood to Mrs. Wilkerson's home but denied attacking her. From what she told the sheriff and what was observed at the crime scene, it was determined that Mrs. Wilkerson had been robbed of sixteen dollars, the amount of cash that John Breeze had on him. This evidence was enough to make an arrest. Three weeks of struggling for life in the hospital finally ended on March 11, 1947, when Mrs. Wilkerson died. John Breeze was charged with first-degree murder and was convicted in a trial in Hillsborough, after the jury took just twenty minutes before coming back with the verdict.

Breeze had been in and out of trouble his whole life it seemed, and when he went to prison for the murder of Agnes Wilkerson, he had no intention of participating in any sort of reformation of character. He was what many of his guards described as "the most stubborn prisoner to enter death row." He had to be forced to do everything, like bathing and eating. He fought the law every step of the way as he worked through appeals and legal requests. He tried to convince the warden that he was insane in the hopes of saving his life, but after several tests, evaluations and interviews with those who knew him, Breeze was deemed sane. John Breeze was scheduled to die the day after Christmas 1947. Governor Gregg Cherry intervened as the date grew closer. An execution the day after Christmas seemed vulgar, and he gave

Central Prison in Raleigh became home to George Alston until his execution for the murder of Helen Massey. *North Carolina Archives.*

Breeze a temporary reprieve. His new date was set for January 17, 1948. Breeze let it be known that he would have to be carried into the gas chamber. He was not going out without a fight.

The night before Breeze's execution, the prison chaplain held a prayer session, which was traditional for inmates on death row before an execution. Breeze attended, and along with the other residents of death row, he sang hymns and prayed with the chaplain. The next day, he was stoic. The fight he promised never came, and Breeze slipped into a silent, somber mood. The day turned to evening, and he was served scrambled eggs and bacon for his last meal. The only words anyone heard him speak all day came when he finished his first plate; he held it out to the guard and said, "Give me some more bacon and eggs." They did, and he finished his second plate with the same vigor he had finished the first with.

A few minutes before 10:00 p.m., he was led into the gas chamber on unsteady legs. He silently, yet intently, watched as the guards as they fastened the straps around his hands and legs. When they finished, Breeze turned his gaze to the small glass partition that separated the gas chamber from the small room where witnesses were gathered. He stared at them as the guards fit the mask on his face, which seemed almost too big for his small body. The guards left the room, and at the stroke of the hour, the executioner dropped the cyanide pill, and the gas began to do its deadly work. John Breeze maintained his gaze on the witnesses, and his frail body did not betray him until the last moment when his muscles tightened, and he fell limp. It took him eleven minutes to die. His body was claimed by his wife, and he was later buried. Mrs. Wilkerson, in her last days on the earth, had been an advocate for justice as she described what had happened to her and identified John Breeze as her attacker. What no one has ever been able to determine is why he committed the crime. Why would he so viciously and sadistically attack Mrs. Wilkerson and try to set her body on fire to hide the evidence of stealing a mere sixteen dollars? The answer to that question died in the gas chamber with John Breeze that January night.

10

FOREST THEATER SUICIDE

The spring of 1950 was in bloom on the campus of UNC as graduate student and part-time economics instructor Ira Castles from Monroe, Louisiana, cut through the trees and foliage on his way to a dental appointment. He would be lying if he had said he was not a little nervous on this simple journey from his home near Gimghoul Castle to town for his appointment. He was well aware of the manhunt that was occurring and the fact that there was a killer on the loose.

The day before, Good Friday, had started out like any other day on the quiet southern campus until the news that there had been a murder on Henderson Street came out. After shots were heard, Leon Smithey, a thirty-year-old ex–graduate student, was seen walking out of a house and disappearing into the bustle of the little village, heading toward the post office on Franklin Street. Upon an investigation of the house, the body of twenty-two-year-old George Bennett Jr. was found inside.

It was obvious from the scene what happened. Smithey and Bennett had opposite rooms in the basement of the white frame house. Smithey had entered the room and shot Bennett in the head. The first shot grazed his head and landed in his arm. Bennett tried to run from the room, but Smithey shot him four more times. A fifth shot missed but was not necessary, as Bennett slumped dead by the door. Smithey calmly stood over his victim and emptied the expended cartridges from the .38-caliber revolver. The empty shells tinged as they hit the floor, and he reloaded the gun before putting it in his pocket and walking up the stairs and out the front door.

A statewide manhunt was called by the North Carolina State Bureau of Investigation (SBI), but it was thought that Smithey was more than likely still in Chapel Hill. Ira Castles had been following the situation like everyone else, and had he not been limited for time to get to his 9:00 a.m. dentist appointment, he would have stayed on the main roads. But he looked down at his watch and saw that it was already 8:50 a.m., and he had to take a shortcut.

Len Smithey may have been suffering from severe PTSD when he murdered George Bennett in 1950. *Chapel Hill Newspapers.*

As he neared the Forest Theater, Ira stopped dead in his tracks. He could see, just a few feet in front of him, a man leaning against a tree. He stood, breathing heavily, suddenly looking at the man. The man looked like he could have been sleeping, but Ira could not fully see him. He called out to him a couple of times as he neared him, but the man did not stir. As Ira came around the tree in full sight of the man, he could see that he was not sleeping at all but dead.

The man had a single hole in his right temple, and in his right hand, he clutched a revolver that lay across his lap. Castles stood in awe and total horror for just a moment until he suddenly snapped out of his trance and broke out in a run toward Raleigh Street. As he emerged from the woods, he made a beeline for the nearest house and used their phone to call the police. Upon arrival, Police Chief W.T. Sloan of the Chapel Hill Police Department was immediately able to identify the body as that of Leon Smithey.

The chief was relieved beyond belief and told the press that they had been searching all the previous day and night for Smithey. He thanked the highway patrol and the SBI for helping with the search. When it came to the many questions about why the crime was committed, the chief was stumped—everyone was, it seemed.

Smithey had previously lived in Chapel Hill with his parents, and when they decided to move when he was just a teenager, he decided to stay on his own to finish high school there. He lived with the Pullen family for a few years, and they considered him family. He worked around town and was well thought of by all who knew him. In 1940, as the nation drew closer to war, Smithey volunteered to join the army. When World War II came, he was a

The Forest Theater. *Author's collection.*

part of the very tip of the spear and saw action on Guadalcanal in the early days of the fighting. When he returned from the war, he took up classes at UNC and moved back in with the Pullen family.

By 1948, however, it was clear that the young man who had left Chapel Hill for the Pacific was not the same young man who returned. Smithey became combative and mean. Finally, the Pullens asked him to find a room elsewhere, and he rented the room in the basement on Henderson Street, where he would later commit murder.

The other people who lived in the house learned to just stay clear of Smithey. Just a few days prior to the murder, people said he became furious with George Bennett and accused him of stealing a rifle that he owned. Bennett denied taking the rifle, but it was obvious that Smithey did not believe him. No one would have thought that he would have escalated the situation the way he did. After the murder, it was revealed that he had spent some time in the veterans' hospital for what we would call post-traumatic stress disorder today and had been released against the wishes of his family. Smithey had been able to go back to Chapel Hill, as a professor vouched for him at the veterans' hospital and promised to keep an eye on him and give him some support.

It is not known for sure why Smithey killed George Bennett, as there was no letter with an explanation left for anyone. It seemed that Smithey had gone straight from the scene of his crime to the lonely tree behind the Forest Theater and taken his life. The murder-suicide rocked the foundations of the small town during both the terrifying eighteen-hour manhunt and the following years. Chapel Hill had rarely known tragedy at that level before, but unfortunately, it would experience it time and time again in the decades following the crime. Whatever illusion the people of Chapel Hill had of things like that not happening in their town was torn down on April 10, 1950. And as men and women dressed their children in their Sunday best for Easter service that year, they had more reason than ever to bow and pray for protection from God, as it seemed like the devil had finally come to town.

11

THE MURDER OF RACHEL CROOK

Highway Patrolman R.R. Thomas was not looking for anything specific as he patrolled the backroads of Chapel Hill on August 30, 1951. It was a lovely rural area in a small town where there was rarely a problem outside of a college student who had partied a little too hard or a traffic accident. He cruised along with his arm out the window, enjoying the warm summer air and the beautiful green grass and trees that lined the road. Suddenly, he saw something near the edge of the trees that caught his eye.

Patrolman Thomas pulled his car over and walked toward the heap of what looked like some kind of debris. As he came closer, he could see that it was not just some old clothes that someone had thrown out on the country road; it was the body of a woman. He stood over the scene and looked down at what was obviously the body of an older female, but beyond that, it was unrecognizable. The woman had been beaten so severely that there was no way to see any human features on her face or distinguish who she was. Her dress had been pulled up, and it was obvious to Patrolman Thomas that she had also been sexually assaulted. He walked back to his car and called in the homicide on his car radio. As he stood there, waiting for backup, he looked around at the gorgeous countryside and shook his head. "What the hell is the world coming to?" he thought.

It didn't take long for the body to be identified once it was taken to the coroner's office. The body was that of sixty-nine-year-old Rachel Crook. The news rocked the small town, as everyone either knew her or knew of her. Rachel had been a constant fixture on the corner of Franklin Street and South Merritt Mill Road at her fish market and remnant store she ran there.

The body of sixty-nine-year-old Rachel Crook was found near the New Hope Presbyterian Church in 1951. *Author's collection.*

Rachel had moved to Chapel Hill in 1930 after a lifetime of academic achievement and service. She was the daughter of Confederate brigadier general David C. Crook of Alabama. She was raised in a strict Methodist household by her father, who, after the war, had become a Methodist preacher. Rachel had been given every opportunity and luxury of a young woman from a well-to-do family of the time. She attended Methodist Junior College in Tuskegee, Alabama, and Vanderbilt University in Tennessee. Rachel became a high school teacher and then taught at Georgia's Lucy Cobb Institute. She went on to continue her education, earning a master's degree in mathematics at Alabama Polytechnic Institute, which later became Auburn University. She had come to Chapel Hill to earn her doctorate in economics from UNC. She had spent the previous twelve years working on her degree and had finished all the requirements, except for her thesis, at the time of her death.

Rachel had moved into a small house that was originally designed as a child's playhouse on the very edge of town, just next to the small town of Carrboro. She was a very interesting lady, and everyone liked her. She was always talking to people and trying to start new businesses at the stand that was in front of her little home.

Immediately, it was thought that the motive for the murder had been robbery, although Sherriff Sam Latta told the press that there were no leads in the days after the murder. Although Rachel appeared to be just a poor older woman, as she sold fish and trinkets from her roadside stand, it was widely known that she was the heir of a very prosperous family in Alabama. In fact, she still owned an 820-acre farm in Union Springs.

Despite the theory about the killer's motive, Sheriff Latta told the truth to the press. The only information the police had was that Rachel had last been seen by passersby at her stand around 7:30 p.m. on Wednesday night. The police searched her home and the lot where her stand was but found no clues. They were confident that she had been murdered that night and dumped on the rural road by her killer or killers, but they had no further leads.

A week after the murder, an arrest was made. Hobart M. Lee, a bulldozer driver from Burlington, North Carolina, was charged with the murder of Rachel Crook. He had been arrested on largely circumstantial evidence that included footprints and tire tracks found at the scene of the crime. The prints and tracks matched those of his green 1949 Ford truck. Lee was questioned by Sheriff Latta, and he told him that he was drunk the night of the murder and could not recall where he was or what he did. Witnesses claimed that they had seen a green truck matching the description of his

Crook's Corner restaurant now stands on the corner where Rachel Crook once sold produce and fish. *Author's collection.*

Old Chapel Hill Cemetery, the final resting place of Rachel Crook. *Author's collection.*

Rachel Crook's gravestone. *Author's collection.*

driving near the place where the body was found and had heard screams coming from the truck.

Although there was strong circumstantial evidence against Lee, it took the jury only an hour and a half to find him not guilty. When the verdict was read, the courtroom erupted in cheers as Lee hugged his wife and mother. The jury found the evidence to be too thin to convict him of murder, and the testimony of Sheriff Latta came into question, as he testified about what Lee had said during interrogation relying on his memory alone instead of using any records from his conversations with Lee. The police kept the case open and waited for some break, but as the years passed, the case got colder.

The intersection where Rachel ran her fish market saw many changes over the years. It was the location of a taxi stand, a pool hall and a bait and tackle shop over the next few decades. In 1978, the building was remodeled, upgraded and turned into a barbecue restaurant called Crook's Corner in Rachel's honor, and it still stands today. Rachel's murder was never solved, and the anxiety the community experienced in the aftermath has long since passed. It is likely that whoever killed Rachel Crook has also passed away or is elderly today. Although the killer is more than likely no longer a threat to the town, there are many who would still like to see justice for Rachel or at least know what happened to her that summer evening.

12
ATTEMPTED FRATRICIDE

Summer was still about a month away, but the sun was shining, and everything was green and fresh in Chapel Hill in May 1954. William Joyner and Allen Long struggled to carry the two cases of beer they had bought for the barefoot party planned at the Phi Delta Theta house on South Columbia Street in Chapel Hill. The beautiful day gave way to a clear and dark night. William and Allen shared a room on the second floor of the brick house with majestic white columns in the front. The party went as they usually did, with music and girls seemingly materializing out of nowhere and then disappearing until next time.

Around 2:00 a.m., William and Allen were joined by another student, Putnam Davis Jr., a twenty-three-year-old art student and fraternity brother. Putnam was a brilliant kid from a wealthy Greenwich, Connecticut family. Putnam was never known to be a talker, but he was especially quiet this night. The three watched a poker game all night and finally settled into their room to listen to records and drink. William and Allen talked to each other and tried to bring their fraternity brother into the conversation as much as possible, but he was so sullen, they finally let him be. The hours ticked by as they listened to Bill Haley and his Comets wail out "Shake Rattle and Roll" over and over.

The sun was already peeking over the horizon and illuminating the campus when Allen decided he had to throw in the towel. He looked around at the empty beer cans by each of the guys. There were dozens of them, but he didn't feel like he had that much to drink. He thought some of them had to leftovers from their other bull sessions. He looked at Putnam, who sat staring silently at the wall, and noticed he had about ten empty cans around him. He figured that he must have drunk more because he wasn't doing any talking. He figured there was nothing to distract him but the beer. Allen walked out of the room as William stretched out his hands and yawned. Allen knew William was done as well and was hoping Putnam would get the drift and head out so they could crash.

Putnam Davis tried to kill two of his fraternity brothers before taking his own life. *Chapel Hill Newspapers.*

Allen finished up in the bathroom and walked back down the hall to his room. As he came through the door, he was met by a jarring sight. Across the room from William sat Putnam, just as he was before, but there was a look of horror on William's face. Allen looked at Putnam and, in an instant, saw that he had a small pistol in his hand and was pointing it at William. In a flash, he fired into William's chest and turned his attention to Allen. Allen turned to run from the room and was shot in the back shoulder and fell forward into the hall. He immediately began crawling away from the doorway, expecting, at any moment, for Putnam to be standing over him to finish the job.

Other members of the fraternity heard the gunshots and rushed to the room. Matthew "Reet" Mason came down from the third floor and saw Allen laying in the hall, wounded.

"Reet, get me to the hospital. I've been shot," said Allen.

Reet knelt down to look at his wounds and heard William yell from the hall bathroom across from his room.

"Brother Davis shot me," William yelled.

Another frat brother joined Reet there in the hall, and they looked at each other. They had heard several shots, but now, other than the groans of their wounded brothers in the hall and bathroom, the room they had come from, there was only silence. One of the students crept quietly against the wall toward the door and peered inside. There, he saw Putnam on the bottom bunk of the bunk bed on the far side of the room. He had a small hole on the left side of his head. A small revolver was still clutched in his left hand, and it was clear he was dead. The brothers called the police, and soon, the exclusive fraternity house was a bustling crime scene. William and Allen were taken to Memorial Hospital for treatment, and the police conducted interviews and took pictures of the shooter. They were told the same thing over and over by the people who knew him. He was sensitive and moody but extremely brilliant. He was going places in the art world, they all said, but he was just not very social. They said he was very quiet guy. The police searched through his room and looked for a letter or diary, anything that would give them any indication about why he tried to kill his fraternity brothers or why he killed himself. They could find nothing.

Putnam's father, Putnam Davis Sr., flew into town as soon as he was asked to collect his son's body and take it home to be buried. Like everyone else, he was at a loss for words. He could not understand why his son would do such a thing. Both William and Allen survived their wounds and graduated from UNC. The experience and the shock of the moment stayed with them for the rest of their lives. The university came out publicly and vowed to address drinking and partying at the fraternity houses on campus, but not much could be done to curtail the young students from having the full fraternity experience.

More than anything, the saddest part of the situation was the unseen force that had a grip on Putnam. It is widely thought that he suffered from severe depression or some other mental illness that was not being treated. There is no way to know if things would have been different if he had sought some help or if someone had recognized that he needed help before that morning. In 1954, mental illnesses were not subjects that had been studied, and they had not been accepted as a real illness.

13

MURDER-SUICIDE AT COBB DORM

The 1960s are looked back on as tumultuous years in American history with the Vietnam War, civil rights marches, riots, hippies, drugs and rock and roll. These things all helped define the decade, but it didn't start out that way. The 1960s began as a continuation of the Americana era that had defined the 1950s. In Chapel Hill, which was always known as a progressive corner of the state of North Carolina, the seeds of the revolutionary eruption of the 1960s grew and were often watered by outspoken professors. The previous decade had opened the eyes of students and residents to the fact that bad things could happen to them in their sleepy little town. The 1960s would cement those feelings.

The lunch rush was starting at Lenoir Hall on October 7, 1961, and cafeteria manager George Prillman was getting concerned. He was not only preoccupied about the growing line of hungry students that he could not serve properly because he was short staffed, but he was also worried about the two young men who were missing from the day's staff. They were always there on time and were solid workers. He broke away from the busy lunch line and went to the phone in his office.

The two missing men were William Johnson Jr., a twenty-four-year-old graduate student from Statesville, and James Barham, a twenty-one-year-old junior from Burlington. They were self-help students who were working for the university to help pay for their tuition, room and board. Both of the young men had great reputations, and their combined absence made Prillman immediately worry that something had happened to them. He knew that Barham was the second-floor dormitory manager at Cobb Dorm.

Cobb Residential Community. *Author's collection.*

The phone rang at Cobb Dorm, and George Prillman asked if the men were there. Robert Holt, the custodian who was working at the dorm that day, spoke to Prillman and told him that they were in their room sleeping. He had just cleaned the room a few minutes before, and they seemed fine and were just in a deep sleep. Prillman felt uneasy and told his staff that he would be back as soon as possible. On the way out, he ran into a university police officer and asked him to go with him to Cobb to check on the men.

When Prillman and the officer arrived, Robert Holt was standing by the door, waiting for them. He had gone back to the room and taken a closer look at the boys. He now thought that they may be dead. Prillman and the officer climbed the stairs to room 201, where they found the two men in their pajamas, lying on their backs, straight as arrows. Blankets partially covered one man's face, and a pillow covered the other's face. They looked closely at the men and found that they were in fact dead and had been for several hours. There was a dried foam around the men's mouths, and their eyes were partially opened. Prillman and the officer questioned Holt, who admitted that it was odd for the men to still be in their rooms sleeping so late, but he said it was not his business to wake them up. He had cleaned as quickly and as quietly as possible and left.

The police came and questioned other residents of the dorm and learned that the last time the men had been seen was the night before. Around midnight, James Barham was in the bathroom at the end of the second-floor hall, getting ready for bed, when he passed out. Several of the other students who lived there carried him to his room, where Johnson met them at the door. "Lay him down here," he told them as he pointed to his own bed, which was nearest the door. The students said they were going to call for a doctor, but Johnson stopped them. "He is fine," Johnson told them. He swore that he would call a doctor if he got worse, but he insisted Barham was fine. They all thought it was incredibly weird, but he was firm. The other students knew the two were close and expected that Johnson would actually call a doctor if Barham got worse.

They had, in fact, found the body of Barham in Johnson's bed, where the students had left him, and found Johnson in Barham's bed. Everyone they interviewed said the same thing about the men. Barham was a friendly person who was easy to talk to, and Johnson was quieter and more withdrawn. A coroner's investigation found that the two had died of cyanide poisoning, although there were no traces of the substance in the room. Their deaths were a complete mystery.

Speculation ran across the campus and the university like wildfire, as people whispered about conspiracies and homosexual affairs. Several events fueled these rumors. The first was the sudden death of Robert Smith Mauldin, a thirty-three-year-old former graduate student who was working as a photographer for the university. He was found dead on his couch the same day the bodies of Johnson and Barham were found. His death was investigated and ruled a natural death from an ongoing illness.

A UNC junior named Ralph Sergeant was arrested for dispensing cyanide pills to another student. He was found in possession of eight mercuric cyanide pills that he said he had gotten in 1959 when he worked in a dental laboratory in North Plainfield, New Jersey, the town he was from. He was cooperative with the police, however, and was deemed to not be connected to either of the students, Mauldin or their deaths.

Lastly, during the police investigation, a chemistry student who had known William Johnson told them that Johnson had asked him the day before the deaths if he knew where he could get a "fast-acting poison." He said he had no idea and thought nothing of it since Johnson was generally quiet and sometimes awkward. His testimony, along with the lack of cyanide in the room and the events of the night of the men's deaths, caused the rumor mill to turn feverishly. The way Johnson reacted when Barham passed out and

Cyanide was used in the murder-suicide at Cobb. *Author's collection.*

the pair's eventual deaths led to speculation that the two were possibly in a relationship that had gone wrong or that they had a suicide pact.

Another speculation is that Johnson was homosexual and had been rebuffed by Barham. He then possibly killed Barham and then himself to protect his reputation, but these are all still just rumors. The last official word on the matter came from the authorities who investigated the matter. They reported that although the crime was not officially solved, they could confirm that the deaths were caused by someone who was in the room that night and was now dead. It is possible that they had more information but did not want to release it to avoid additional pain or embarrassment for the dead men's families.

14

A CHRISTMAS TRAGEDY

Around noon on Christmas Eve 1963, Alfred Foushee was finishing up some last-minute Christmas shopping in downtown Chapel Hill when he ran into Frank Rinaldi. Alfred had done some general housework for Frank in the late summer and was not at all excited to see him. Frank was with another man, so Alfred hoped he did not notice him, but sure enough, their eyes met before Alfred could make his move to leave the shop without being noticed. When Frank noticed Alfred, he did not greet him or smile. What he said turned Alfred's blood cold and made him regret seeing Frank even more than he could have ever imagined. "It is over. I did it," Frank said, and he passed Alfred by with his companion following behind. Alfred stood, momentarily stunned, and then hurriedly finished his business in the store before going home to spend Christmas with his family.

Alfred tried to push down the memories of the time he had spent with Frank Rinaldi. He had been hired to do some general cleaning and work for Frank, and he had been asked back several times after that first day to do other jobs. Things became progressively more uncomfortable each time Alfred went to Frank's apartment. It really became a nightmare when, one day, Frank told Alfred he would like to hire him to kill his wife, Lucille. Alfred had never seen her and was only aware of her existence because Frank had told him he was married. Frank lived in the apartment alone as far as Alfred knew.

Alfred refused the offer to murder Lucille, but Frank persisted. As time went by and Frank realized that Alfred would not do the job himself, he offered him $500 just to find him someone else who would do it. Most importantly, Frank told him he was to find someone who could do it and make it look like an accident. Alfred again refused. The last time he had seen Frank Rinaldi, Frank made very aggressive sexual advances toward him and even asked Alfred to expose himself before offering him money for sex. Alfred refused, and Frank apologized, even telling him that he was ashamed of himself for his actions as Alfred left. That was the last time Alfred saw Frank before that day in the store.

Little did Alfred know that as he settled in for his Christmas celebration with his family, across town at Frank Rinaldi's apartment on 105 North Street, the police were walking through a horrible crime scene that they had been called to by Frank Rinaldi's friend John Sipp. There, police found the body of thirty-two-year-old Lucille Rinaldi, five months pregnant and brutally beaten in the face and head, in the small living room of the apartment she shared with her husband, Frank. A sock had been stuffed in her mouth, and a scarf tied around her head kept the sock in place. A blood-covered pillow sat near her on the floor, and the police deduced that she had been smothered with it.

There was no sign of forced entry, but Lucille's pocketbook was opened and its contents strewn on the floor nearby. A bent flashlight was found and determined to be the weapon used to bludgeon her. She was not sexually assaulted, although she was in her pajamas and a housecoat, and it seemed like nothing was missing. To the police officers, it seemed like an obvious attempt to stage robbery, as there were still valuables in the house. Their attention immediately turned to her husband, Frank, as the prime suspect, and he was arrested.

The detectives who investigated the murder found that Frank Rinaldi was an interesting—if odd—man. He, like his wife, was from Waterbury, Connecticut, where they had met years before. He had graduated from Georgetown University in 1951 and taken a job with the CIA. In 1953, he enlisted with the army to serve in Korea during the war. In 1956, when he got out of the army, he moved to Chapel Hill but left a year later to teach at the University of Missouri. From there, he worked with an advertising firm in New York City.

By 1960, he was back in Chapel Hill, where he was working on his doctorate and teaching English as a graduate assistant. He proposed to Lucille in the spring of 1963, and she moved to Chapel Hill with him, where she took a job teaching at Guy B. Phillips Junior High School. She worked just one day at the school in September when school started but then resigned, citing

Frank Rinaldi, twice acquitted of the slaying of his wife, Lucille, lived the rest of his days under a cloud of suspicion. *Chapel Hill Newspapers.*

"extreme personal family trouble," as her reason for leaving the position. She moved back in with her parents in Waterbury while Frank remained in Chapel Hill.

The police found that although their marriage seemed obviously strained, Frank depended on Lucille financially for some time. She had sent him several checks, sometimes up to $200, to support him while he lived in Chapel Hill before they were married. Frank had taken out a $20,000 insurance policy on her, naming himself as the beneficiary. Since Frank named himself as her fiancé on the application, the policy also had a rider allowing for another $20,000 to be dispensed to him if her death was accidental. The letters sent from Frank to Lucille seemed more conciliatory after the policies were bought, and he began to ask her to come back to Chapel Hill.

In the few months leading up to the murder of Lucille, Frank had also taken out several loans from the University Loan Fund for students and from Carolina Bank Trust Company. The investigators found that he had made inquiries about his rights to any inheritance that Lucille was due in the event of the death of her parents. When the police talked to Alfred Foushee, they felt they had the damning information they needed for the district attorney to get a conviction.

Although it seemed that the trial would be little more than a formality, Frank Rinaldi was able to navigate through two separate trials and be acquitted in both. During the first trial, his lawyers argued that the police had not conducted a thorough investigation and had focused on Rinaldi as a suspect instead of trying to follow the process of investigation to solve the crime. They felt that it was more likely that a thief had been surprised by Mrs. Rinaldi and killed her to keep them from being implicated in the robbery. There was also the testimony of John Sipp, who had been with Frank all day on their shopping trip. Sipp was a great witness and was able to recall very minute details about their time together that day. Sipp and his wife had dined with Frank and Lucille the night before the murder, and

Mrs. Sipp testified that she did not see anything to indicate any turmoil between the two.

Many believed that Frank Rinaldi had escaped justice. It is theorized that he was a homosexual who, at the time, may have felt inclined to remain closeted. It's said that when Lucille found out about his sexuality, she returned to Connecticut to think about what she was going to do. She was over thirty years old, newly married and pregnant. Frank, having been discovered, began to find ways to both eliminate Lucille so he could keep his secret and get a financial windfall from the insurance.

There is no way to prove this, of course, as so much time has passed, and Frank Rinaldi was found not guilty in the case of Lucille's death on two separate occasions. But doubt remains to this day, as there seems to be so much evidence that Frank had a hand in his wife's death and there has never been any other suspect identified. Unfortunately, Lucille and her unborn child have never received justice, but their memory remains for those who knew them and for those who were involved in the case.

15

THE UNSOLVED MURDER OF SUELLEN EVANS

The serene southern college campus in Chapel Hill was green and growing on the last day of June 1965. A picture-perfect day welcomed the few students who were attending the university for summer classes. Buses and cars still buzzed up and down the streets of the small town, but there was an emptiness in the air without the thousands of students who would flood the campus in the fall. Then there would be a constant flurry of activity and sound all around the town in diners and bookshops, but that day in June was quiet.

Suellen Evans, a twenty-one-year-old student from Mooresville, North Carolina, walked briskly toward the entrance of Coker Arboretum. She was in a hurry. Her time in Chapel Hill was limited, since she was only going to be there for the summer. A home economics major who had just completed her sophomore year at Catawba College in Salisbury, Suellen was there trying to make up some credits for the next step in her academic career. She had recently been accepted to the University of North Carolina in Greensboro and wanted to make sure she was on track. She was a friendly brunette who, although she had come to Chapel Hill just a short few weeks before, had made several friends.

Suellen shielded her eyes as she looked both ways down East Cameron Street before crossing over. As she reached the other side and the shade of the oaks surrounding the iconic Old Well cleared her vision, she saw a friend from class. They chatted for a moment there, but Suellen could not tarry. She had a bus to catch in just a few hours that would take her back home to Mooresville for the weekend. She was not antisocial and regretted not staying with the other girls in her dorm over the weekend, but in her heart, she knew there was no place like home. Even for a young lady who herself sought more than the standard experience of girls her age at the time—getting married and having kids—she still loved to go back home as often as possible.

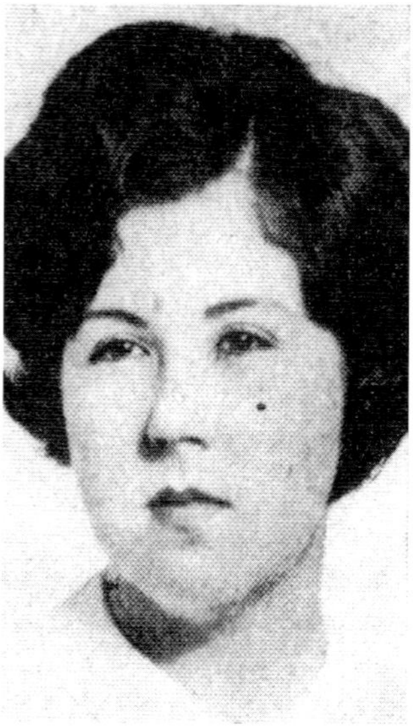

Suellen Evans was the victim of a brutal murder in the Coker Arboretum. *Chapel Hill Newspapers.*

Suellen ended the conversation with her friend by letting her know that she was in a rush. She had to stop by Alumni Hall to ask one of her professors a question before the weekend and had to get back to her dorm to pack. She crossed McKorkle Place, carefully dodging the squirrels who darted about and fed on the acorns as if the people were not even there. She could see the bustle of Franklin Street through the trees as she passed the Old East building and bounded up the steps of Alumni Hall. The meeting with her professor was quick, and as she exited the other side of the building, she felt content that she was doing well and that making the journey home was not going to put her behind in her studies.

She looked down at her watch; 12:30 p.m. stared back at her. She needed to make sure she packed and made it to the bus station on time. She was staying in Cobb Dorm, so the quickest way back was a shortcut through Coker Arboretum to Raleigh Street. She headed toward the entrance of the arboretum, looking forward to seeing the pretty foliage that grew there and the birds that flitted among the bushes and small trees. She had never been anywhere as lovely as Chapel Hill in the summertime, she thought as she walked along the path. Her swift gait and determined pace moving through the overgrown arboretum was suddenly stopped as she was grabbed by an assailant who sprang from the bushes and dragged her back into the foliage.

Suellen fought as hard as she could against her attacker, and her screams were heard by passersby. A female student heard the screaming, as did a pair of passing nuns on Raleigh Street. They could tell the sound was coming from the arboretum and bravely ran toward the screams. Suellen was winning her fight for freedom against the predator and almost broke free from him. Sensing he was losing his prey, he lashed out with a knife, slashing her neck

The Coker Arboretum. *Author's collection.*

and stabbing her in the heart. As she made her final move toward freedom, the coed who was coming to her aid saw her stumble from the bushes into the path and then collapse onto a bed of periwinkles. Her blue-and-white-striped homemade shirt was torn and stained with blood. As Suellen fell, the student was sure she saw a dark arm grasping at her legs, but it soon disappeared into the bramble. The nuns were right behind the coed and leaped toward the falling Suellen as she collapsed by the path. The female student peered through the green leaves and flowers of the arboretum to see if she could spot the attacker, but he had vanished.

One of the nuns knelt beside Suellen and cradled her head. She looked up at the nun and said, "He tried to rape me....I think I am going to faint." With that, she lost consciousness and never opened her eyes to the blue sky again. An ambulance from North Carolina Memorial Hospital arrived just a few moments later, but it was too late. Suellen was not going to make it back home to Mooresville. She was not going to be able to see her parents or ever attend the University of North Carolina at Greensboro.

The police descended on the arboretum and immediately sealed off the area. They had a few immediate leads, one about a Black man who was working as a janitor at the time. He was walking out of Phillips Hall when

The dense foliage that hid Suellen Evans's killer. *Author's collection.*

The entrance to the Coker Arboretum from Country Club Boulevard. *Author's collection.*

the police arrived near the arboretum, but he was soon released. Another passerby said they had seen an older red-haired white man leave the arboretum around the time of the murder, get into a '61 or '62 Rambler and drive away. The witness said the man had stains on his shirt that may have been blood, but the police could find no other witness who had seen the man or any suspect who fit that description.

The student body at UNC banded together and raised $1,285 as a reward for anyone who had information about the crime. Over 200 men came to Chapel Hill to help search the area for any weapons or clues that would help solve the crime, but nothing was found. Over the next five years, the police followed 251 leads and interviewed 116 suspects from Chicago, Illinois, to Odessa, Texas. All these leads and these suspects came to dead ends. The Chapel Hill Police Department was never able to close the case or bring anyone to justice for the senseless death of Suellen Evans. She was killed just as she was beginning to spread her wings to fly—a true tragedy.

16

THE SENSELESS MURDER OF OFFICER TED COLE

Ted Cole was enjoying a summer day off on June 4, 1969. It was a beautiful day, and he was spending it working in his yard. Cole had been a Chapel Hill police officer since 1965 and was considered one of the best men on the force. His wife was proud of him and watched him out the window on that sunny Wednesday afternoon as he worked in the yard. Suddenly, the idealistic scene was disturbed by the abrupt squeal of brakes as a car came to a sudden stop in front of the house. Out of the car came a man carrying a shotgun. He advanced across the yard toward Cole and yelled, "Why you tell them damn lies on me?" He raised his shotgun to his waist and fired. Ted Cole fell where he stood, and the man walked up to him and reloaded the shotgun. He then fired into Cole as he lay on the ground. Cole's wife screamed in horror and ran to call the police as the man got back in his car and sped away.

Amos Baldwin was drunk. He had been drinking for days. The married father of seven children seemed to always be drunk at the time. His wife had always been frustrated with his behavior, and she tried her best to raise their children. Even the job Amos had at a local church did not seem to straighten him out. He had been arrested several times for things like speeding and carrying a concealed weapon. Although Baldwin had been arrested by several different officers, he had been arrested by one officer more than once: Officer Ted Cole.

Baldwin began to blame most of his troubles on Officer Cole. He began to talk around town about what he intended to do to him. More than once, Baldwin told people that he was going to kill Cole. In the days leading up

Officer Ted Cole was known as one of the best officers on the force at the time of his death. *Chapel Hill Police Department.*

to June 4, Baldwin was spiraling. His wife would later testify that he looked like something was wrong with him. It scared her. On the day of the murder, he picked up his distant cousin Ralph Baldwin and headed toward Chapel Hill.

Ralph would later testify that they made several stops that day. One stop was Marley's Barber Shop, where Ralph borrowed five dollars from one of the barbers who worked there. Then they drove to a gas station, where Amos asked the attendant where Officer Minor lived. (Amos did not know where Ted Cole lived, but he had been told he was a neighbor of Chapel Hill police officer Minor.) The attendant told Amos where Minor lived, and the pair were off again in Amos's blue Ford Falcon.

They ended up in Carrboro, where they got tags for the car, and then Amos took some pills. Ralph was not sure what the pills were, and even Amos would later testify that he was not sure what he had taken—but he did say that he did not remember what happened after he took them. Ralph told the police that Amos drove to Officer Cole's house on Piney Mountain Road and saw him in the yard. Amos had a folding shotgun and a .22-caliber pistol in his car. Amos sped up and came to a sudden stop in front of the house where Cole was working. Amos jumped out of the car, and Ralph watched as Amos gunned Cole down. Amos ran back to the car, and the pair sped away as Ralph listened to the screams of Ted Cole's wife grow fainter as they gained distance from the house.

But Amos Baldwin was drunk, and soon, he ran the car into a ditch and wrecked it. The pair then got out and started walking. The two men were picked up and dropped off at Amos's house. Ralph left and went straight to the police to report the crime. The police were already on the lookout for Amos, and he was soon spotted riding with two men in Chapel Hill. They found him in the car with Clyde Maynor and Everett Smith in front of the Town and Country Shopping Center. Eight officers from the Chapel Hill Police Department surrounded the car the three men were in. Baldwin had the shotgun with him, and although he threatened the officers, he did not put up a fight. This was great news for the startled Maynor and Smith, who found themselves in the middle of Amos Baldwin's endgame.

Amos Baldwin stood trial in Hillsborough for the murder of Officer Ted Cole. *Author's collection.*

Baldwin was booked for first-degree murder and taken to Cherry Hospital in Goldsboro for a mental evaluation. When it came time for the trial, the prosecutor did not want there to be any questions about Amos's sanity at the time of the killing. Also for the trial, the jury had to be brought in from Person County to avoid any prejudiced feelings against Baldwin affecting the verdict. Cole had been a good man and a great officer. Most of the people in town knew him, and interest in the case had been widespread across Orange County. During the trial, the jury heard Baldwin's claim that he did not remember what happened, but they also heard the testimony of several other people who said Baldwin had told them multiple times that he was planning on killing Cole. One person even testified to hearing him say that they would be reading his name in the paper soon.

After hearing all the evidence from the prosecutor and the defense attorney, the jury convened and began to formulate their verdict. When they came back, the verdict said Amos was guilty. He was sentenced to life in prison. The prosecutor had ended his closing arguments with stirring words that struck home: "When Amos shot Ted Cole down like a dog, he shot down the very fabric of this country….Are we going to say a man can go out and get drunk and do anything he wants?" His words put the onus on the jury to decide whether, even if they did believe Amos was so intoxicated that he did not know what he was doing, that justified him avoiding justice. They thought not.

17

STORM TROOPERS MURDER

By 1970, America was dealing with a new birth of freedom for many marginalized groups who had fought hard during the 1960s to have a voice. These new freedoms brought with them backlash from many Americans who craved the days when these groups existed only in passing on the street and not in their neighborhoods and schools. Universities became tinderboxes for clashes over the Vietnam War and race-related conflicts across the country, and tensions ran high. Even in Chapel Hill, where many reveled in the progressive nature of the university, there were many local residents who were not always so forward-thinking.

Locals called James Cates "Baby Boy." He was not a large man, but he was handsome and a sharp dresser. Sharper than his appearance were his wit and humor. Cates was twenty-two years old on November 21, 1970. As he danced the night away in the early morning hours at the union on UNC's campus, he had no idea that he had such a short time left to live.

Cates had grown up in the Northside neighborhood of Chapel Hill, a Black neighborhood in what was still a very segregated South. He loved to play baseball and spent a great deal of time in at the Hargrave Community Center, playing with his friends. He also loved to dance, so when the union and the Committee for Afro-American Studies planned an interracial dance on campus to promote integration and help race relations, he was excited. He met his friends in front of G&N Grill on Rosemary Street, and they made their way through campus, eager to hear the Dorvells, who had just finished a southern tour and were back in town.

The dance started at midnight and was supposed to go until 7:00 a.m. Unfortunately, an altercation took place earlier that evening between a few young Black people at the dance and a group of Nazi-themed bikers who called their gang the Storm Troopers. A fight broke out in front of the union, and the dancers flooded out into the crisp November air to see what was going on. The lone police officer on site came out in time to see a biker and several Black students fighting. As he approached, yelling for them to stop, the Black students ran off into the night, and he grabbed the biker. The biker was yelling that he was going to "kill some niggers" before the night was over. The officer tried to hold him as more members of the biker gang and Black students began to break out in fights.

Another officer responded, but they could not contain the melee that was taking place. The largest fight occurred in the area known as the Pit, where ten to twelve young people and five gang members brawled. More officers arrived in time to disperse the crowd. As people stepped away and the police took control of the situation, it became apparent that someone had been seriously injured. James Cates lay on the bricks, holding his stomach in a pool of blood. The police called for an ambulance but stood watch around the area, as if they were waiting for another fight to break out at any minute. A former army medic rushed to James's side and tried to stop the bleeding from the gash on his stomach. There was blood everywhere, which hid the smaller stab wound in his groin that had cut his femoral artery and was causing him to bleed out.

The crowd began to yell at the police to do something. The ambulance was taking too long, and the hospital was only about a mile away. When some people stepped forward from the crowd and attempted to take James to the hospital themselves, they were stopped by the police. The police told the crowd to leave him where he was until medical personnel could get there and take over, but it soon became evident that they would not get there in time. Finally, the police took James and put him in the back of a patrol car and made their way to the hospital, where the doctors found him barely clinging to life. A nurse tried to give him an IV but found that he had lost so much blood that his veins were deflated. James began to flatline, and although they tried to resuscitate him, they were unable to, and he died.

The police were widely criticized in the Black community for the way they handled the young man's murder. When the fight was initially dispersed, the police told the Storm Troopers to leave, probably in the hopes of sending the problem away so the young people could get back to their dance, which had been uneventful until they showed up. In the

The Pit, where the fight between James Cates and the Storm Troopers took place. *Author's collection.*

process, they sent away a murderer and lost any chance of asking any questions or speaking to any witnesses who could identify the killer on the spot. The length of time the police waited to take James to the hospital was disputed. The police claimed they took him after waiting for just fourteen minutes, but the witnesses claimed they waited at least forty-five minutes. Every minute was valuable for James, and the delayed care in a hospital may have been the final cause of his death. The crime scene was cleaned almost immediately, which caused an uproar, as it eliminated that much more evidence that may have led to a prosecution.

After the incident, three members of the Storm Troopers were charged with second-degree murder and tried, but the lack of evidence and the lackluster performance of the prosecution led to a not guilty verdict from an all-white jury. Evidence was presented that showed, during the fight, James had pulled out a straight razor, so the defense introduced a theory of self-defense for the bikers. Because of the size of the crowd, the dark surroundings and the fact that many had been drinking and many were fighting, the jury ruled in the bikers' favor.

The Black community in Chapel Hill could not help but see the vast difference in response from the town for the murder of Suellen Evans just five years before and the murder of James Cates. When Suellen was killed, the town came together and mobilized all its resources to find the killer. But when James died, there was almost no reaction from the community at large. The not guilty verdicts enraged many in the Black community, and the night of the verdict, there were two firebombs set off in Chapel Hill. One was placed at the Institute of Pharmacy on Rosemary Street and the other at the Chapel Hill-Carrboro School's Administration Building on School Lane. No one was arrested for these bombings, but when there were three more bombings a few weeks later, seventeen arrests were made, all young Black men and women who were almost all from the Northside neighborhood. Ironically, although no one went to prison for the slaying of James Cates, four of the young men who were arrested for the firebombing spent years in prison for their involvement.

18

FRANKLIN STREET DRIVE-BY

When the 1970s came to a close, the nation seemed almost exhausted from nearly two decades of counterculture and revolution. The "New Right" had found a new audience with the many people who were tired of the constant upheaval of the 1960s and 1970s. Chapel Hill was still a bastion of liberal thought, but the new reality of the conservative leanings of the nation crept into the reality of the school and would find a foil in classrooms and lecture halls for the next two decades. But as the 1980s dawned, there was still a crisp feeling of newness in the air in Chapel Hill.

It was supposed to be a kind of bachelor's party for Jerry, and he was about as rambunctious as he would allow himself to get before his May wedding to his fiancée, Peggy. They were both seniors at UNC and were busy making plans for the future. Jerry Hodge was twenty-four years old and finishing up a degree in education. He was looking forward to a career teaching American history to high school students.

On the night of February 3, 1980, Jerry, Peggy and his cousin and roommate attended a basketball game and were having a great time. At around 2:00 a.m., Peggy decided she was done, and the group walked her to Winston Dorm, where she lived. But the men were not ready to throw in the towel yet and decided to head to Hector's Restaurant on the corner of East Franklin and Henderson Streets.

As the three men walked through the quiet and cold campus toward a hot meal, they began to play around and toss snowballs at each other while dodging between trees and between parked cars. Staring down the barrel of full adulthood, they took this opportunity to play as if they were little boys again. It was a great night, and they were having the most fun they'd had in a long time until Jerry launched a snowball at his cousin and missed, hitting a silver and red Chevy truck. The door immediately opened, and the dome light came on, revealing that the cab of the truck was full. Two men and two women were in the truck, and the driver was stepping out, cursing as he came.

Jerry tried to calm him and down and apologize, but the aggression shown by the man rankled him. As the argument escalated, both men were restrained by members of their parties. The angry man got back into his truck and drove off as Jerry and his group continued walking across campus toward Hector's.

Public Safety Officer Ron Downey was sitting in his car on East Franklin Street when he saw the men cross the road, walking away from him. He gave them a cursory glance and assessed them as no threat. They looked cold and were walking close to each other with their hands in their pockets, trying to stay warm. He figured they were just looking for something to eat like all the other kids who were out on Franklin Street at this time of night. As they crossed in front of the post office, Downey's attention was aroused once more when he saw a red and silver truck turn on the street in his rearview mirror. The truck passed him, and he could see that it had four people in the cab. It went by him slowly, but he could tell the passengers did not notice him in his cubby where he was parked. The truck did not arouse any sense of danger in him either. They had too many people in the cab, but it was too late and too cold to pull them over and bother with who was taking who home.

Suddenly, shots rang out in the night. Officer Downey looked up to see an arm hanging out of the truck, firing a pistol at the group of men who had just crossed the street. Two of the men scattered, and one fell straight down. Officer Downey hit his lights and immediately began following the truck.

On the street, Jerry Hodge lay bleeding profusely. He had been shot in the back with a 9-millimeter pistol, and the bullet had come out of his chest. He was rushed to Memorial Hospital, where he died a little over an hour later. Officer Downey had no trouble overtaking the silver and red truck that sped away and was not resisted by its occupants.

In the truck, he found twenty-four-year-old Robert Harry Groves Jr. and three other passengers. He was not a student of the university and was just in town for the night, hanging out. He lived in Roxboro and worked at Carolina Power and Light Company. Groves explained to Officer Downey that he

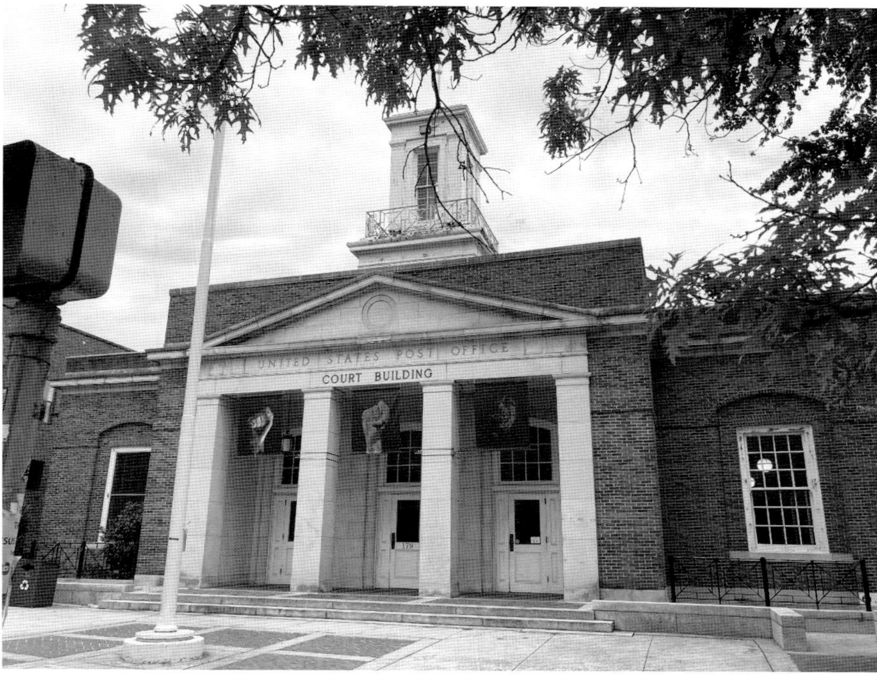

Above: Jerry Hodge was shot down in front of the post office on Franklin Street in the cold of an early February morning. *Author's collection.*

Right: The group of friends was heading to Hector's, which is now the home of the famous Time-Out restaurant. *Author's collection.*

had a confrontation with the other men about a snowball or a piece of ice being thrown at his truck, and he was just planning to shoot at the group but did not intend to hit anyone. No matter his intention, he was arrested and charged with first-degree murder. His passengers were allowed to leave.

The phone rang after 3:00 a.m. at the Hodges' home in Waynesville, where Jerry's parents were asleep. The news was beyond anything they could have considered. Peggy was told what happened and found herself lost in sudden and total sadness. Her hopes, dreams and future plans were shattered in an instant over a snowball. Robert Groves was not a criminal prior to that moment of pride and rage that overtook him early that morning. He took a plea deal to avoid the death penalty. He pleaded guilty to second-degree murder and was sentenced to life in prison. This brief moment of senselessness changed the lives of many that night, including Groves's.

19

WRONG PLACE AT THE WRONG TIME

Thomas Perry Zimmerman was a senior at UNC from High Point, North Carolina. He was a good guy and loved to just hang out. On the night of February 4, 1985, he was hanging out with one of his buddies, Robert Wimberly, at his trailer at the Hilltop Mobile Home Park in Hillsborough. They were there with Zimmerman's two roommates, William Bullock and James Young, who were sitting around the small kitchen table while Zimmerman sat on the couch, strumming a guitar. Suddenly, the door to the trailer burst open, and a man wearing a ski mask came in, waving a gun and yelling for everyone to get down on the ground. The men around the table jumped at his command, and the table shook as they complied, raining empty beer cans and cigarette ashes on the floor. Zimmerman also complied with the assailant and got down on the floor in the living room as the man with the gun stood over him.

The gunman fired a shot into the ceiling. "Where's the stuff?" he yelled. "Where is it?"

"What stuff?" rose a voice from the floor as another man entered the trailer. "What are you talking about?" said another.

Wimberly had recognized the first man immediately when he entered the trailer, even before he spoke. He recognized the man's body and the way he walked. Wimberly almost said his name out loud but thought better of it. When Steve Sanders entered the room unmasked, there was no doubt that the first man was Richard Sanders. Richard had spoken in his regular voice when he came in, but when his brother Steve came in, he tried to disguise his voice with a falsetto, Mickey Mouse–sounding tone. But no matter what he did, it was too late; Wimberly knew exactly who he was dealing with.

Steve and Richard Sanders were brothers from Pittsboro, North Carolina. They had both been in trouble before. Steve was wanted for breaking into cars in Carrboro, and Richard was on bond for a robbery with a deadly weapon he committed the previous November. On the night of February 4, the brothers, along with another man, stopped by Tijuana Fats in Chapel Hill, where Steve worked, and spoke to some of his coworkers. "Where could we score some cocaine?" was the question of the night. They couldn't get a good answer, so they headed north of Chapel Hill to Hillsborough, where Richard had bought some cocaine before from Robert Wimberly.

They were there for drugs, and they meant to have them. The Sanders brothers began to take turns beating the men on the ground with a piece of wood while the other ransacked the house. Blow after blow rained down on the prone men as they tried their best to shield themselves from the beating. All the while, the Sanders brothers kept yelling, "Where is the stuff?"

"Stop looking at me!" one assailant yelled at Zimmerman as he walked past him lying on the living room floor.

"I'm not looking at you! I'm not looking at you!" Perry said as he buried his face into the carpet.

The men in the kitchen could hear them each time they traversed the living room area. "Quit looking at me!" Then came the swish and thud of the wooden club as it came down on Perry.

The two robbers, after finding only a small amount of marijuana in the house, rifled through the men's pockets and took their money and car keys. They went outside to search the cars. The four men lay on the floor, beaten and bloody but terrified to make a move. After a few minutes of quiet in the house, Bullock called out, "Are you gone? Are they gone?" To his horror, a call came back from right outside of the door in response.

"Hell, no we ain't gone. We're going to kill you!"

None of the men in the kitchen saw which of the men it was, but one of them came back into the house and went into the living room where Zimmerman was. They heard a shot ring out, and they heard Zimmerman cry out in pain; then came the footsteps and quiet again. It took a few minutes before the men got the nerve to stir from their spots and venture into the living room, where they found Zimmerman facedown in a pool of blood. Robert Wimberly moved his head out of the way to make sure he was alive and would not suffocate on the blood. They called the police and an ambulance, but it was too late for Zimmerman.

The Sanders brothers were captured a few days after positive identifications from the men in the house. They had also received testimonies from friends of the Sanderses and a man who had ridden with them that night but stayed in the car during the robbery and murder. James Youngman had recognized Steve Sanders when he came into the trailer because they had gone to high school together. Robert Wimberly recognized Richard Sanders because he had sold him drugs on several occasions. When the brothers could not score any drugs earlier in the night, it seems they planned to go to Robert's house to take his supply, which, at the time, he did not have. The brothers were sentenced to life plus fourteen years in prison. Thomas Perry Zimmerman never got the chance to graduate from UNC or the chance to find his place in this world.

20

MURDER AT THE INTERNATIONALIST BOOKSTORE

Bob Sheldon was supposed to spend the evening hanging out with his friend Ken after work on February 21, 1991. He spent the last few hours before closing tidying up and organizing the books and magazines that filled the small store on Rosemary Street. It seemed like a normal night in Chapel Hill, but halfway around the world in the sky over Iraq and Kuwait, United States military jets flew combat missions against the invading forces of Iraqi dictator Saddam Hussein.

In August the previous year, Saddam Hussein had ordered the invasion of Kuwait in response to Kuwait's refusal to forgive war debt incurred by Iraq during the Iran-Iraq War of the 1980s. The move had been provocative to say the least and had led to the destabilization of the region, threatening the world's oil supply. The world mobilized behind the United States to face the threat, and President George H.W. Bush gave Hussein an ultimatum: get out of Kuwait or face the consequences. The Iraqi dictator refused, and by late February, coalition forces were several weeks into an aerial bombardment of Iraqi forces.

For the most part, the American public was standing behind the president's decision, and he enjoyed record-high approval ratings during this time. After the deep emotional scar of the Vietnam War, the country was swept up in a feeling of deep patriotism, and American flags were everywhere. Vietnam veterans who had gone to war and come home to protestors and hateful rhetoric led the way in supporting the young men and women who were serving in the Persian Gulf.

Bob Sheldon was a rebel to say the least. In fact, it can be reasonably said that he was an anarchist at heart. He was known for going against the grain and raging against the machine. He had resisted the draft during the Vietnam War, visited China, supported the Communist Workers Party and done some union organizing. He moved to Chapel Hill in the mid-1970s from Colorado and first worked in the Cone Mills Textile plant; he then worked as a nurse at the UNC infirmary on campus. He also worked with the Youth Brigade of the Revolutionary Communist Party and often wore a red beret around town.

By 1981, Sheldon had opened Internationalist Books. It was a small reading room above a bar on Henderson Street that was filled with Marxist and communist literature. In time, the location became so popular that he moved it to a larger location on Rosemary Street. Most days, he could be found there, talking to patrons about politics.

Always outspoken, Bob Sheldon became the focus of anger when he came out strongly against the war in the Persian Gulf. Many of his friends became concerned when he escalated his rhetoric from just speaking with patrons in the store to organizing protests and teach-ins against the military buildup. After the bombing started, when American soldiers were in harm's way, he appeared on the local news, speaking out against the war.

That night in February 1991, Ken Kaye arrived at the bookstore to find his friend Bob Sheldon lying in a pool of blood on the floor by the front counter. He quickly called 911, and Bob was rushed to the hospital, where he fought for his life for twenty-four hours before he was pronounced dead. Bob had been shot in the head, and the store's cashbox was missing, which made the murder appear to have been motivated by robbery. The Chapel Hill Police Department searched the store and spoke to as many people as they could but found few clues and nothing that would give them a solid lead to a viable suspect.

Friends of Bob did not believe that the murder was the result of a robbery. They knew that if Bob had been confronted by an armed robber, he would have given up any money that was in the store without any resistance. He was totally unmotivated by money, and there was always a meager amount in the cashbox at any time. They were more inclined to believe that the murder was motivated by the intense patriotism the community was experiencing and Bob's pushback against the sentiment.

Unfortunately, Bob was teetering on the brink of death when he was found and was never able to communicate with the police or anyone at the hospital to give them any indication about who committed the crime.

The body of Bob Sheldon was found in his bookshop, Internationalist Books, which was located in the building where Mama Dip's is today. *Author's collection.*

The case remains unsolved, although many in Chapel Hill have tried to keep Bob's legacy alive. Through volunteers and workers, Internationalist Books stayed in business, despite a couple of location changes, until 2016. Even though the store has closed, Bob Sheldon is still remembered in the activist community in Chapel Hill, and he was even immortalized in the song "Chapel Hill," by the band Sonic Youth. Maybe one day the case will have a break that will lead to the arrest of Bob's murderer, but until then, people will remember the true anarchist Bob Sheldon who was a contrarian to the very end.

21

THE BUTCHER OF MINCEY ROAD

The police investigators stood around the remains of a smoldering fire in the yard of a white farmhouse on Mincey Road, just north of Hillsborough. Looking down into the ashes, where gray ash and partially burned wood mixed with orange, glowing embers, they saw something else, something that none of them had seen before. The charred black remains of a human torso smoked and burned there in front of them, along with what appeared to be charred lungs and other human organs. They stared silently until the moment was broken by movement in their peripheral vision, which made them all look up. A dog ran across the yard with a human hand in its mouth. The nightmare scene was straight from the pages of a horror novel, but it was far too real. Investigators moved into the house to investigate and found a human ear on the rail of the porch. Inside, other human ears were found in the freezer, and one was even found in a fruit bowl on the counter. In the refrigerator was a jar that contained severed testicles.

These were found at the home of David Sokolowski, an occasional roofer who lived in the house with his girlfriend, Pam Ellwood, who was nowhere to be found. The only clue about her whereabouts was an earring in one of the ears that was found in the house. News of the findings rocked Orange County and made statewide news reports. Rumors of cannibalism and witchcraft were rampant. The sheriff's department had more questions than answers and needed to speak to the occupant of the house. He was not hard to find and was soon sitting across an interrogation table from the sheriff's investigators.

Unimaginable rumors of cannibalism emanated from Mincey Road in Orange County. *Author's collection.*

David Sokolowski had been a model child, handsome, polite and smart. It seems everyone who had known him since childhood thought the world of him. David and his brother were adopted as infants and raised in Durham. His parents were caring and smart, giving the two every opportunity to be successful. David's brother John ended up becoming an accountant living in Atlanta. David was on the right track until his teenage years, when he was introduced to drugs and alcohol. It was a turning point in his life. He was arrested for the first time at the age of seventeen, and his criminal activity escalated over the next few years. While serving a long term at Central Prison in Raleigh, he met Rubel "Little Man" Hill.

When David got out of jail, he reconnected with Rubel, and they became neighbors on Mincey Road. David and Rubel spent a great deal of time together, drinking and doing drugs. David Sokolowski was known to be a mean drunk and would start fights and become violent. He was cruel, once killing Pam's cat and severing its head, leaving it on the porch for her to find. In mid-February 1992, when Pam disappeared and David told everyone she had left him, it made sense to many.

On March 8, 1992, Pam's parents drove in from Winston-Salem, North Carolina, to see about their daughter, whom they had not heard from in several weeks. Pam's mother and father knocked on the door, but there was no answer. They started to walk around back when they came face to face with David, who was carrying a shotgun and had a pistol sticking out of his pocket. Startled, they asked about Pam. David told them that she had gone to town with his friend Rubel's wife, Leann, and that they would not be home until after dark. Dejected, they got back in their car and drove back to Winston-Salem. As they pulled out of the driveway, they saw David dragging wooden pallets and stacking them in a pile in the backyard.

When the investigators interviewed Sokolowski, he told them that he and Rubel had gotten into a fight and that Rubel had pulled a gun on him. He said he then killed him in self-defense. However, evidence showed a different story. In the remains of the burnt torso that belonged to Rubel Hill, the coroner found many gunshot wounds from a pistol, as well as a shotgun blast directly into the back. It was apparent that he had been gunned down. And what about Pam? The police asked David about her, too, but he claimed ignorance. He said she left him—that was it.

DNA evidence showed that the remains in the fire were Rubel's, but the ear with the earring belonged to Pam. The house and the grounds were searched, but other remains were never found. The investigators believed that Pam had tried to leave David sometime in February, after the last time she had been seen. They believe David killed her and burned her remains after mutilating her body. Around the time her parents came looking for her, it is believed that Rubel found out about the murder and was going to call the authorities about David, so he killed him, too. The massive fire that almost completely destroyed the remains of Rubel "Little Man" Hill had most likely finished off any remains there might have been of Pam in the fire pit.

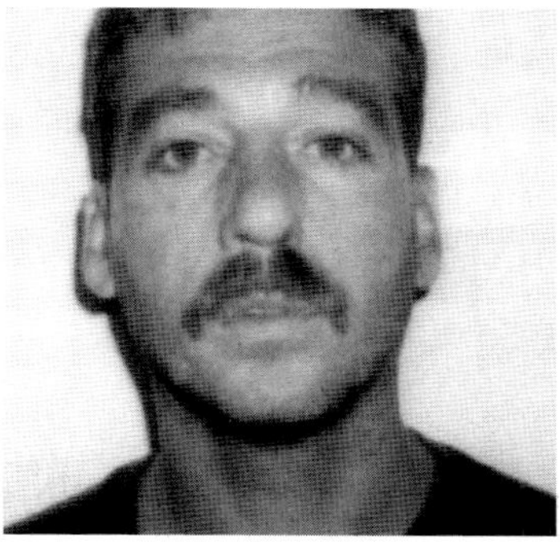

David Sokolowski. *Mugshot.*

David Sokolowski was convicted of the murder of Rubel Hill and received a life sentence. He was further convicted of the murder of Pam Ellwood and received another life sentence that was added on the first. He will never again walk the Earth as a free man, but he will live. He received life in prison but doled out death sentences to his victims so callously and cruelly. He shined a light on that country road in the northern part of Orange County and proved that evil can exist anywhere at any time.

22

A FATHER'S LOVE

The car's headlights cut through the night as they got closer to their final destination. George Holman Jr. and his brother Randy were looking for the Oldsmobile Cutlass of Kevin "Buck" Nickens, who they heard was at the Burger King in Carrboro. It was a little after midnight on June 3, 1993, and George's heart was pounding. He never thought he would be in this position, but he was at his wit's end. He was a family man. He loved his wife, Delia, and son George Holman III, or "G.J.," with all his heart. The seasons of life come and go, and he was nearing that time when his seventeen-year-old son would graduate high school and move out, leaving him and his wife alone once again.

The previous few months had tried his family like none before. His son had dated a girl who, like a lot of other girls, had an ex-boyfriend. And the ex-boyfriend, like a lot of other ex-boyfriends, was upset by this. The difference was that this young lady's ex-boyfriend was a known gang member and drug dealer in the Carrboro and Chapel Hill area. It seemed like nineteen-year-old Kevin "Buck" Nickens was constantly in trouble with the law. People who knew him would tell you that he had been a "mama's boy" in his youth and had a good mind but had taken a turn in his adolescent years to crime. By that night in 1993, he had been arrested over forty times for crimes including assault, speeding, carrying a concealed weapon and possessing cocaine with the intent to sell. In 1992, he had been sentenced to three years in prison for possessing cocaine, driving with a revoked license and carrying a concealed handgun on the campus of Chapel Hill High School. However, he served only three months of the sentence at the Sandhills Youth Center in McCain before he was back on the streets in Chapel Hill.

Every officer in the Chapel Hill Police force knew Nickens by sight, and they had all had some form of interaction with him. G.J. was a good kid and a basketball player who wasn't looking for any trouble. But trouble found him, and he began to come home with stories of harassment and threats from Nickens. For months, this carried on. G.J. didn't take the threats lightly and neither did his father, who worried constantly that his son may be caught up in the violence that permeated the streets of the larger nearby city of Durham that flooded the news each night. In May 1993, George took G.J. to the magistrate to swear out a warrant for Nickens, claiming he had shot at him but missed. By the night of June 3, 1993, the warrant had still not been served.

George and his brother Randy had set out to confront Nickens and plead for him to leave G.J. and the family alone. It had gone on long enough. They found Nickens on Graham Street, but the conversation turned into a confrontation, with police having to separate the men. Nickens drove off in his Cutlass and disappeared into the night. George and Randy got back into George's Camry and cruised the streets of Chapel Hill and Carrboro, looking for Buck Nickens. They found him at Burger King. As the Camry pulled into the lot, Buck looked up from a conversation he was having with two girls in another car to look at Holman. George Holman jumped from his car, and words were exchanged. A heated and tense moment seemed to stop time for the briefest of moments. Then George Holman pulled out a pistol and began to fire at Nickens, who ran toward the restaurant. Nickens found the doors locked as he fled from George Holman, who followed behind Buck, firing into him. Buck ran around the side of the Burger King and made it to the drive-thru before he finally fell. George Holman ran back to the car, where Randy waited and sped off. George threw the gun into University Lake on his way home.

Nickens was still alive and conscious when the police and EMTs arrived. He identified his attacker before he faded, and he died at 8:15 the next morning. He had been shot twice in the abdomen, once in the chest and once in the right thigh.

Holman was arrested without incident that morning and charged with first-degree murder. When people from the community heard of the slaying, a divide emerged. Everyone who knew George Holman could not believe it. He was such a good man that they felt if he committed this crime, he must have felt he had to do it. When they found out the crime was connected to threats made against George's son, the news solidified in their support for George. Buck Nickens was also a known pariah to many in the community. It seemed to many like a clear meeting between good and evil and good fighting back.

On the other hand, many who knew Nickens had a much different perception of him and the situation. They pointed out his rough upbringing and the fact that, to his family and friends, he was loving and loyal. They felt that he had been caught up in a system that had driven him further and further down the wrong path. They also felt that even though he was not a model citizen and had been involved in crimes, this did not mean his life was worthless. Even the Carrboro chief of police was quoted in the papers as saying that "it was just a matter of time" with Nickens.

At the trial, George Holman testified that when he confronted Nickens at the Burger King, Nickens said he was going to kill G.J. and his entire family. He said that Nickens had appeared to go for a gun when he began shooting. The prosecutors accused Holman of going to the Burger King with the intent to kill Nickens. In the end, the jury convicted Holman of manslaughter, and he was sentenced to six years in prison. The jury empathized with his feelings as a father and took into account the high degree of pressure he was under, fearing that harm would come to his son. Many felt that justice was not served and that George had coldly gunned down a young man who had not been given the chance to grow out of a wild stage in his life.

23

THE ASSASSINATION OF BUCK COPELAND

The judge looked out over the courtroom and then at the jury foreman. "Has the jury reached a verdict?" he asked.

"Yes," the foreman answered.

The silence of the courtroom was soon broken by the reading of the verdict and the answer to the affirmative by each member of the jury. "Guilty, murder in the first degree."

David Allen Lewis turned stoically to the Orange County deputy and held his hands out, wrists together, as if to say, "Cuff me." It had been a long and strange road that led him to that moment, and still, everyone involved had more questions than answers about why a man whom all would have described as quiet, hardworking and pleasant to be around had done such an awful thing.

That awful thing occurred on Wednesday, September 14, 1994, around 9:00 a.m. James "Buck" Copeland walked into the McDonald's restaurant on Franklin Street, where he often got breakfast. It was just next door to Yates Motor Company Inc., where Buck was a vice-president and the general manager. Some days, he ate at the Hardee's restaurant close by, but he felt like eating at McDonald's that day and ordered his food and coffee with a smile. He took his tray and took a seat where he usually sat and drank a sip of coffee. It was a beautiful day as he looked out the window at the people walking by. It was also his sixty-first birthday. Buck Copeland unwrapped his breakfast and raised the coffee cup to his lips—then it was over.

David Lewis took his fate stoically at the Orange County Courthouse. *Author's collection.*

What he had not seen was David Lewis lurking in the shadows of the restaurant. When Lewis had seen Copeland come in, he had gotten out to his truck and come back in carrying a sawed-off .410 shotgun. He walked straight up to Copeland as he drank his coffee. "Oh, you're not going to talk? Oh, you don't remember me, do you?" Lewis said as he walked up to Copeland, raising the shotgun in his hands. Before Copeland could react, he put the gun to the side of Copeland's head and pulled the trigger. Buck Copeland slumped in his chair and slid to the floor as the customers and employees of the restaurant looked on in horror.

Lewis momentarily looked down at his victim and then calmly turned and walked out the door. Two men who had been working on a car in the parking lot saw him exit and walk slowly to his gray Mazda truck, open the door, throw the shotgun on the seat beside him and pull out of the parking lot like nothing happened. Had a woman not run from the restaurant as the truck pulled onto Franklin Street and pointed at the truck yelling that the driver had just killed a man, the men never would have known they were looking at a killer.

The police were immediately called and dispatched to the restaurant, where they found Buck Copeland dead on arrival. The search for the killer started but did not last long. As the police swarmed the McDonald's and began the process of interviewing witnesses and securing the crime scene, a gray Mazda truck pulled into the Chapel Hill Police Department lot and parked. David Lewis got out of the truck and walked in the front door. He asked the desk officer if he could speak to an investigator, and he sat quietly and patiently in the lobby until someone came to speak to him. When they did, they heard his confession of the crime, and he was arrested on the spot.

Yellow tape went up around his truck, and the shotgun was found on the seat inside. The police had the killer, David Lewis. They had the murder weapon, a sawed-off .410 shotgun with a pistol grip. They had everything they needed to convict, but they didn't know why the crime had been committed. Lewis was not giving them anything regarding a motive. The police found out that he had worked at Yates for Copeland but had left in February. He left of his own accord and had not been fired. Everyone they spoke to said he was a good worker and was happy there. He worked there changing oil, driving around customers who had left their cars there and doing some detail work. The only change they noticed came after he gave his notice. Jobs he had once been happy to take on, he balked at. Things

The McDonald's on Franklin Street was once the scene of a cold-blooded murder. *Author's collection.*

After David Lewis committed murder, he drove to the Chapel Hill Police Department and calmly turned himself in. *Author's collection.*

he would gladly do before when asked would get a response from Lewis of, "That's not my job." Still, even with the attitude change, Lewis left on good terms.

There was much speculation that Lewis had done work for Copeland and had either not been paid or felt slighted in some way. There was also a rumor that Lewis had bought a Nissan from Yates and was behind on his payments. Many thought Copeland was leaning on him for the payment and had threatened him with repossessing the car or ruining his credit. In both cases, nothing was ever verified. There was no record of Lewis doing any work for Copeland and not being compensated, and the records showed that Lewis had made his payments for the Nissan on time and was up to date.

When the trial came, Lewis's attorney presented a defense of "residual schizophrenia." Lewis had a record of some mental health issues. His wife and other family members confirmed that he was a very quiet and withdrawn person. In 1986, he had jumped from a bridge and was hit by a car in an attempted suicide. After the incident, he suffered devastating headaches. His defense presented the theory that Lewis had, at some point, gotten the idea that Copeland had wronged him and developed a warped obsession with him. His attorney asked for leniency in the judgment against Lewis in a bid to save his life. As the trial came to a close, the jury overwhelmingly did not buy this defense. A lone holdout in the jury for a lesser charge eventually acquiesced to the other jurors, and Lewis received a sentence of life in prison. The holdout juror later came out and claimed she was pressured into the judgment but confirmed her vote of guilty when called on in the reading of the verdict.

24

FAILED JUSTICE

Ralph Walker walked out the front door of the rooming house where he was living in Chapel Hill on January 26, 1995. At the age of forty-two, the divorced father of three had taken a job at McDonald's as a manager trainee and was on his way to work when a shot rang out, and he fell on the front steps of the house, dead. His killer, dressed in a green army jacket and armed with a World War II–era M1 rifle and a knapsack filled with six hundred rounds of ammo, moved to his next victim.

As he moved down Henderson Street, UNC student and lacrosse player Kevin Reichardt rode by the shooter, unaware of the danger he was in. The stalker raised his rifle and shot the young man off his bicycle. Kevin tried to crawl away from him, but the shooter stood over him and shot him dead as he was on the ground. People began to recognize what was happening and started to scatter and hide as the shooter moved farther down the street, crossing over Rosemary Street and heading toward Franklin Street, where he was sure to come upon more victims.

Suddenly, a Chapel Hill police car appeared, driven by Officer Demetrise Stephenson, who did not initially see the shooter. She had received a call of gunshots but had no idea of the seriousness of the situation or the location of the shooter. The shooter saw her first as she slowly turned onto Henderson Street, scanning the area. He crouched low and moved toward her car. By the time she recognized the danger, it was too late to respond. Her eyes widened and her face contorted in horror as the killer brought his rifle to his shoulder and fired into the driver's side door. The

Above: Wendell Williamson stalked down Henderson Street on a shooting rampage in January 1995. *Author's collection.*

Opposite, top: Williamson engaged police in a gun battle at the intersection of Henderson and Rosemary Streets. *Author's collection.*

Opposite, bottom: The terror came to an end after a student ran through a hail of gunfire and tackled Williamson. *Author's collection.*

shot ripped through her left hand, and she slumped down in the car seat. He moved toward her to finish the job, but luckily, at this moment, other officers arrived on the scene.

A gun battle began, and the shooter, hit in the leg and wounded, remained on his feet and continued firing. In a flash, he stopped to reload his weapon, and a twenty-six-year-old UNC student, former marine and Gulf War veteran named Bill Leone appeared out of nowhere and tackled the assailant. Fifty-year-old attorney Bob Epting jumped into the fray and helped Leone wrestle the gun away and detain the shooter as the police came in for the arrest. Leone was shot by the police accidently as he rushed the shooter, but he survived. The shooter was taken into custody, and the police set out to find out who he was and why had he done what he did.

Rosemary St
Henderson St

It was not long before they knew the shooter's identity. They called him "Rambo" down at the Henderson Bar & Grill where he liked to hang out, drink beer and get into debates with other patrons. His real name was Wendell Williamson, and he was a law student at UNC. Police found that he had been seeing a physiatrist since he had been arrested for yelling at students and hitting himself in the face until he cried.

Williamson was tested and found to be afflicted with paranoid schizophrenia. His lawyers used this fact to argue that he had not been mentally capable of realizing the consequences of his actions. He was charged with two counts of first-degree murder, but in November 1995, he was committed to the Broughton Mental Institute, where he would be evaluated every year to see if he was still a danger to himself or others. He would never go to prison or answer for the murders he committed that February afternoon, which left the victims' families and loved ones shocked and outraged.

To add insult to injury, Williamson sued the university for not providing the right level of care to him while he was a student at the law school there. His attorneys argued that he had been seeing a psychiatrist who had retired and not turned him over to another doctor for proper care. They argued for Williamson that he would not have committed the crimes if he had been receiving the proper care. The judge agreed, and Williamson was awarded $500,000. He was also allowed to write a book about his mental illness and sell it freely, the proceeds going to an appointed nonprofit. To this day, the book can be purchased, and the victims' loved ones still have to deal with the knowledge that Williamson still ticks off his years and works toward one day leaving the hospital and becoming a free man.

25
THE BOY UNDER THE BILLBOARD

It was still warm in North Carolina on September 25, 1998. Although the leaves were beginning to give up and fall from many of the area's trees, summer was still king for another month. The North Carolina Department of Transportation kept the roadsides tidy and cut, but it was a constant battle, with summer storms dumping water on the grass and feeding it as it reached for the sky, growing faster than anyone could keep up with. In Mebane, a small town along I-85 on the west side of Chapel Hill, a crew went about their business, cutting the tall grass down the side of the highway, when they came upon the skeletal remains of a child under a billboard. The police and medical examiners descended on the location and went to work.

The remains were those of a young boy. The police examined the scene and deduced that he must have been killed somewhere else. The area showed no signs of struggle or any activity at all. The boy was wearing khaki shorts, white socks and new black and white shoes. In his pocket, police found fifty dollars, which puzzled them. Why would the killer leave the money, no matter why they had murdered the boy? The skeletal remains led them to believe that the boy had been killed sometime during the summer of 1998. Remnants of straight, dark brown hair indicated that the boy had a light brown to fair completion and brown eyes. At first, the police felt that he may have been a Hispanic child. The area was heavily agricultural, and the use of migrant labor was common. It was thought that he was most likely the child of migrant workers, and that may have been reason they had no report of a missing child. No one knew it at the time, but the pieces to the puzzle that would identify the boy under the billboard and solve his murder were already there—only time and technology stood in the way.

On May 13, 1998, a few months before the boy was found, further south on I-85, near Spartanburg, South Carolina, a man was walking along a service road, picking up cans. The roar of traffic drowned out the more pleasant sounds around him, but that was not what he was there for. He picked up the cans to turn them in for cash. Every little bit helped. Around 1:30 p.m., he was getting hot and tired but went on looking until there, in the tall grass beside the road, he found the nude body of an Asian woman. The investigation of her death found that she had ligature marks on her wrists, showing that she had been tied up and had struggled against the rope. Her cause of death was deemed to be suffocation. She was unidentified, and the crime was unsolved. The two bodies found along this busy interstate shared a secret that was known only to them, their killer and God. This unidentified woman and boy were mother and child.

The unsolved case of the young boy whose body was found callously discarded in the tall grass beside the road in Mebane captured the imaginations of many residents, and he became known as "the boy under the billboard" on the nightly news when any bit of information was shared. For one Orange County Sheriff's Department investigator, Tim Horne, solving the murder became an obsession. For the next twenty years, a box of records and evidence would sit under his desk as he worked his cases. Years came and went. Cases were solved and closed, but the box remained, and occasionally, he would take it out and look through the documents and pictures to try to find something he may have missed—something that may break the case.

Decades passed, and the case remained unsolved, despite the efforts of many. Forensic sculptor Frank Bender created a bust of the boy using the skull that was found. Time and technology progressed, and the sails behind the case finally caught wind when Barbara Rae-Venter, the genetic genealogist who found the link that led to the capture of the Golden State Killer using DNA and ancestry records, got involved with the case. She found that the boy found was in fact biracial, having a Caucasian and Asian parent. A distant relative was also found living in Hawaii. Investigator Horne was back in business, and after following the leads and speaking to the relative in Hawaii, he was led to a closer family in Ohio, where he was able to learn once and for all the identity of the little boy who had lived in his mind for so many years.

His name was Robert "Bobby" Whitt, and in 1998, he was ten years old. His mother, Myoung Hwa Cho, and father, John Russell Whitt, moved together to Charlotte, North Carolina. Soon after moving, Whitt told his family in Ohio that Myoung had gone back to her native South Korea and taken Bobby with her. The family had spent years trying to find them but had come up empty-handed, even after hiring a private investigator and two law firms to help search for the pair in South Korea. Little did they know, all the answers they needed were in a box under a desk in Hillsborough, North Carolina.

Searching for Whitt was easier than the police expected, since he was serving a long prison sentence for robbing ATM users at gunpoint, and he immediately confessed to murdering Bobby and Myoung. They had moved to Charlotte, and he had taken a mistress who wanted to move in with him. Whitt confessed to taking Myoung out and suffocating her with a towel, then driving down to Spartanburg, South Carolina, and dumping her body. This solved the case that the Spartanburg Police Department had been investigating for decades. Whitt moved his mistress into his house and told her that Myoung had gone to South Korea and left him and Bobby.

Soon, the woman began to quarrel with Bobby and wanted him to leave, too. John Russell said he tried to make them get along but to no avail. She wanted him to send Bobby to be with his mother in South Korea. John Russell Whitt knew that this was not an option, so one day, he drove Bobby to a storage facility and told him they were going to play a game. He told Bobby to get into the back seat, where he suffocated him with a towel, just as he had done his mother, and drove him to the billboard in Mebane, where he dumped his body.

All the pieces were finally together, and John Russell Whitt was sentenced to fifty-two to sixty-four years in prison that were to begin when his sentence for the armed robbery was complete in 2037. Tim Horne and the family of Bobby and Myoung received some solace in at least knowing what happened to them. The family had always hoped that they could reconnect with their relatives in South Korea, but the news dashed these hopes. But they were able to find closure in the solving of the case and could finally move on with their lives. Investigator Horne, who had retired by the time the case was solved, retrieved the ashes of Myoung from South Carolina and drove them to the family in Ohio, where Bobby's remains were interred next to those of his grandmother. Horne could not stand the thought of the ashes arriving via FedEx to the grieving family. Hopefully, the act allowed some closure for him, as he also spent many years wondering and working to find answers.

26

HIGH SCHOOL KILLER

It was May 14, 2005, and no one had heard from James Sapikowski or his wife, Alison, for several days, which was odd. It was odd enough for a family member to call the Chapel Hill Police Department to conduct a welfare check on the couple. Pamela Powell, Alison's sister who usually spoke with her at least once a week, found that she could not get in touch with Alison at all. After she left her a message on Mother's Day and still didn't hear from her, she was concerned enough to make the call to the police. The police went to the Sapikowskis' 5,700-square-foot home, rang the doorbell and looked in windows but could not get any answer. The officers knocked on the door of their neighbors and were told that they had not seen James or Alison coming or going from the home in several days. The couple had two grown sons and a daughter who was a freshman in college at Washington and Lee University in Virginia. They also had a son named Adam who was in high school and lived with them.

"Has anyone seen Adam, their youngest son?" police asked the neighbors, who said they had also not seen him in a few days. Pamela Powell had been trying to get in touch with him also but had not been able to. His girlfriend lived in the neighborhood, however, and the officers soon found her and asked her a few questions. It didn't take them long to track down the sixteen-year-old Adam Sapikowski, who had checked into a Courtyard by Marriott hotel in Durham a few days before. The police called Adam's older brother who lived close by and asked if he would accompany them to the hotel to try to find him. When they arrived at the hotel, they found Adam in his room.

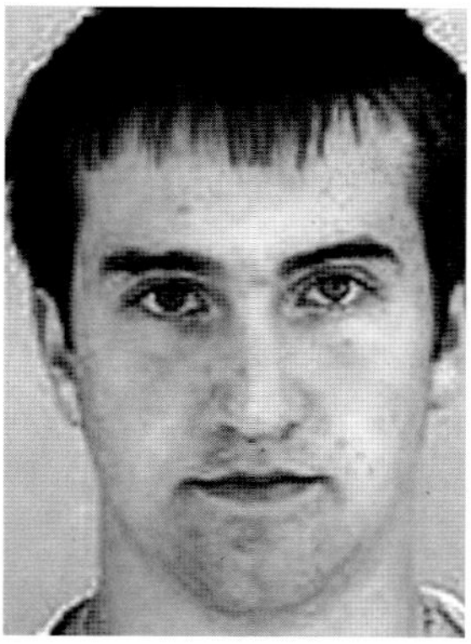

Adam Sapikowski killed his parents and then went to the prom. *Mugshot.*

The police asked Adam to escort them back to the house, and they asked him some questions as they drove from Durham back to Chapel Hill. Adam told them that his parents had gone to El Paso, Texas, to visit his oldest brother, Jim Jr., and his family. This was a red flag to the police since Jim Jr. had not heard from them either, and Alison rarely traveled with her husband. The police heard alarm bells going off when they arrived at the home and Adam told them that he did not have a key to the house. They knew there was no way that parents had left him there by himself with no way to get in and out of the house. The police left Adam by the car with his brother and found a door that could be opened by jimmying it with a credit card on the side of the garage. They crossed the garage and entered the house through the kitchen, where they were met with the smell of death. The officers proceeded up the stairs and looked down the hall into the master bedroom. In front of the door, chairs were stacked, and towels were stuffed under the door. The police backed down the hall and went back to the car to avoid disturbing what was obviously a crime scene.

The officers called in investigators, who arrived and began taking pictures and securing the scene. When they removed the chairs and the towels, they found that the body of James Sapikowski was wrapped in a blanket and lying on the floor in a pool of blood. He was dressed in workout clothes and had been shot in the chest, head and neck. The coroner would later say that any of the shots would have been fatal alone. A trail of blood led investigators into the master bathroom, where the body of Alison was also found wrapped in a blanket, lying in a pool of blood. She was dressed in her nightgown and had been shot in the shoulder and the head. It appeared that she had been shot in the shoulder first, and since this did not kill her, she tried to flee. There was an unused shell beside her body, a gruesome indicator that her killer had stood over her to finish her off and had another shell just in case she lived.

When the investigators walked back to the car and confronted Adam, he confessed to killing his parents two weeks before on April 28. He was arrested and charged with two counts of murder. His family was absolutely appalled and cut off all contact with him immediately. The lavish life he had been living ended abruptly in the cold gray prison cells he haunted while he waited for his trail to begin. He had no financial support, so a public defender was assigned to handle his case. The teenager who had driven an almost-new Chevy Tahoe to his private, $16,000-a-year school that served sushi and Thai food for lunch had brought himself to a position so low that he could not have imagined it. The court decided to charge him as an adult, so the threat of spending the rest of his life in that gray tomb was real.

The murder was so perplexing for the family and everyone who knew them. James, or "Big Jim," as he was called by many, was an active member of the community in Chapel Hill. He was known as a big, affable guy who was generous. Big Jim was the volunteer head coach for the club hockey team in Chapel Hill and was known for buying hundreds of tickets to give out to youth hockey players across the triangle area of Raleigh, Durham and Chapel Hill to try to build interest in the sport. Alison was also active in the community and was regarded by all as a dedicated mother and wife. They were high achievers, and their children were as well. Anyone who was looking from the outside in would say that they had provided all they could for their kids to be successful. The couple's two older sons were already successful adults. Lauren was doing well as a freshman at Washington and Lee University in Virginia. But what about Adam?

Adam also would have been seen as a fine young man before the murders. He ran cross-country and had never been in any kind of trouble. He had a girlfriend and made good grades, which served as the catalyst for the murders. When Adam told the investigators what happened that day, he said it was all the result of a mediocre report card and pressure from his father. According to Adam, he was confronted by his father about his falling grades and the fact that he was spending too much time with his girlfriend and not enough time studying. Adam claimed his father came after him with a baseball bat and said he was afraid he was going to kill him with it, so he shot him. A bat was found in the house, but there was no indication that James had ever beaten Adam with a bat, and his other children categorically deny experiencing any abuse.

Adam said he shot his dad in the kitchen and then moved on to the bedroom, where his mother was. He shot her and then wrapped her body and that of his father in blankets. He dragged his father's body upstairs and his mother's into the bathroom. He then stuffed towels under the bedroom door and stacked chairs in front of it. Adam then went about his business, and the next morning, he went to school like nothing had happened. That weekend, he got dressed up and went with his girlfriend to his prom. Adam even invited several of his friends over to his house after the dance. When they questioned him about the smell of rotting meat in the house, Adam said that the refrigerator was out and that some food had spoiled. It was not long the after party that Adam moved to the hotel. When the police searched his car, they found that he had packed food and camping equipment. He had running on his mind but had decided to stay. His girlfriend told the police that he had asked her to go away with him but she refused, and police believe that is what kept him from fleeing.

While waiting for his trial, Adam claimed he was suicidal, which prompted the authorities to move him from prison to Umstead Hospital in Raleigh, where he could be watched more closely. He also claimed to prison physiatrists that he had been hearing voices since he was in middle school and that he was just acting on what they told him to do. His public defender tried everything from accusations of abuse to pleas of insanity at trial to no avail. He could see that his client was not going to be able to wiggle his way out of a guilty verdict, so they took a deal. Adam pleaded guilty to felony obstruction of justice and the second-degree murder of his father and was sentenced to twenty-four and a half years in prison. He also pleaded guilty to the second-degree murder of his mother, for which he was sentenced to another twenty years in prison, which would not begin until he completed the sentence for his father's murder.

At his sentencing hearing in January 2008, Adam cried and held his head low, avoiding eye contact with his family, who took turns reading impact statements. He said he was sorry, but his apology did not convince any of his former loved ones. After the sentencing, they immediately petitioned the court to block Adam from receiving any inheritance from his parents' estate. They wanted to make sure he did not find himself living a lavish life of leisure somewhere in the distant future once his sentence was up. He is so young that even if he serves the entirety of his sentence, he will still be young enough to enjoy an early retirement. This is a luxury that most people don't get to enjoy, and his parents certainly won't. The judge agreed, and Adam Sapikowski found himself alone and destitute. Only Adam knows why he murdered his parents, but the blood-spattered report card that was found leads most to believe that his father was threatening him with something like taking his Tahoe, not letting him see his girlfriend as much or not allowing him to go to his junior prom. This theory makes you wonder whether it was worth it for Adam, as he now lies on a prison cot while his peers got to go to senior prom and basketball games. He will be in prison when they graduate from college and get jobs. He will be in prison when they get married and have children. He seemed to have it all, but for a long time to come, he will be in prison with nothing.

27

THE KILLING OF EVE CARSON

At five o'clock on the crisp spring morning of March 5, 2008, a call was placed to 911 saying that gunshots and a woman screaming had been heard in the Hillcrest area of Chapel Hill. The Chapel Hill Police Department responded by sending an officer to check the area. As he pulled his car into the intersection of Hillcrest Road and Hillcrest Circle, he saw the lifeless body of a young lady illuminated by his headlights. Upon closer investigation, he could see that she had been shot several times and was covered in blood. The officer called his discovery in, and immediately, investigators descended on the scene. As the sun climbed over the horizon, they were already on the trail of the young woman's killers.

They soon learned the body was that of Eve Carson, UNC's student body president. Eve was a go-getter from an early age. Born in Athens, Georgia, in 1985, she had been an excellent student throughout her youth. Eve had attended Clarke Central High School, where she was the president of that school's student body, valedictorian and vice-president of the school's chapter of the National Honor Society. She volunteered as a tutor with abused and runaway teens and worked at the University of Georgia as a lab assistant, conducting stem cell research. She had chosen the University of North Carolina over many other schools and had excelled there as well. She volunteered with many philanthropic groups in Chapel Hill and continued to be one of the school's top students. Eve was a Morehead Scholar, and in 2007, she became the university's student body president. By all accounts, Eve was a wonderful young woman with a very bright future ahead of her.

The intersection where the body of Eve Carson was found. *Author's collection.*

A quiet neighborhood in Chapel Hill awoke to the news of a vicious murder. *Author's collection.*

The police tried to keep as much information as they could out of the media but also recognized that they needed to use the public to guide the investigation. The police decided to go to the media to get a piece of evidence out into the public to fish for leads. Once they identified Eve Carson as the victim, they began to look into her activity on the day she was murdered. They found that her ATM card had been used in the early morning hours on the day of her death. They also obtained grainy black-and-white security camera images of a young Black male using the card while in an SUV with two passengers who were obscured by the darkness in the backseat. Police released the image to the media, and it had just the effect they were hoping for.

A few days after the pictures began circulating on the local news, a woman named Shanita Love contacted the Chapel Hill Police Department, claiming to have information. The information she gave them led them to the arrest of Demario Atwater and Laurence Lovette Jr. By the time the case went to trial, the police had gained enough information to gain convictions for both men for Eve's murder, and they had a clearer picture of what happened to her that early March morning. Jayson McNeil, a friend of Laurence Lovette, got a call asking for a ride to Chapel Hill to rob someone. McNeil did not go with him, but Lovette later told him what happened that night.

Laurence Lovette told McNeil that he and Demario Atwater had taken his mother's car to Chapel Hill, where they drove around looking for a victim. Unfortunately, Eve Carson was spotted by the duo in her house, tucked away on a side street, in the early morning hours of March 5. They rushed into her house and forced her into the backseat of her Toyota SUV at gunpoint. Lovette got in the driver's seat, and Atwater got in the back with Eve. She cried and tried her best to reason with them as Atwater held her hostage and fondled her. They drove to several ATMs, where they withdrew $700 in total. She begged them for her life, telling them to take whatever they wanted from her, but they showed her no mercy. When they tried to withdraw money from an ATM in Durham and it would no longer allow them to steal money from Eve, they decided she had to die. They drove her to a wooded neighborhood, and Eve came to the realization that her time on Earth was short. Sullenly, she asked them to pray with her as they came to a stop at the crossing of Hillcrest Road and Hillcrest Circle.

The men pulled Eve out of the car, and Lovette shot her five times with a .25-caliber pistol. She fell to the ground but was still alive. Demario Atwater walked over to her and stood over her, looking down on her as she lay dying. He shot her in the head with a sawed-off .410 shotgun as she raised her hands in vain to protect herself from the shot. A few days after the murder, Shanita Love, who lived in an apartment in Durham with Demario Atwater and his family, saw the pictures on her television and later accompanied Atwater, his brother and Laurence Lovette to dispose of the murder weapons. A few days later, Love gave this information to the police, and the arrests were made.

The men were tried separately. Demario Atwater pleaded guilty to federal charges of carjacking, kidnapping and weapons possession on April 19, 2010, and then pleaded guilty to first-degree murder on May 24, 2010. By doing this, he avoided the death penalty and was sentenced to life without the possibility of parole. Laurence Lovette pleaded not guilty to all charges and went to trial. On December 20, 2011, a jury found him guilty on all counts, and he was sentenced by the same judge who sentenced Atwater to life without the possibility of parole. Both men are now serving their sentences in federal prisons. Atwater is serving in California, and Lovette is in North Carolina.

Eve Carson is gone but has not been forgotten. Her life has been honored in many ways since her untimely murder at the hands of these monsters. The University of North Carolina has established a scholarship in her name and dedicated a garden to her near the campus YMCA in Chapel Hill. There is no way to know just how far she could have flown in this world. There is no way to measure the loss that the world experienced that morning. Eve seemed destined for greatness, and the only thing that is certain is that a beautiful young life was taken too soon. Like a shooting star that burns out, the night becoming just a little darker in its absence, the world is a little darker today without the light that Eve Carson gave.

28

HATE CRIME

A little after 5:00 p.m. on February 10, 2015, newlyweds Deah Shaddy Barakat and Yusor Mohammad Abu-Salha were just sitting down to dinner with Yusor's sister Razan Mohammad Abu-Salha. Deah was a second-year dentistry student at UNC, and at the age of twenty-three he had a bright future ahead of him. His wife, Yusor, had just graduated from North Carolina State University in Raleigh and was also planning to attend the dental school at UNC. Yusor's nineteen-year-old sister, Razan, was an undergraduate student at North Carolina State University and was majoring in architecture and environmental design. They were all laughing and smiling as they sat down, but when the doorbell rang, their mood quickly changed. They knew who it had to be.

Deah told them to stay in the kitchen, and he crossed the room toward the front door. In the living room, he took out his cellphone and activated the camera to document what he knew was going to be another confrontation. As he reached the door, the knocking and ringing reached a fevered pitch. He opened the door and found his tormentor there. Craig Hicks was a pariah at the Finley Forest Condominiums in Chapel Hill. He was horribly rude to everyone but had special vitriol for the young Muslims. When Deah and Yusor moved in, Hicks watched them pass by in disgust, staring at their hijab head scarves and commenting to them that he didn't like the way they looked and that they should "get out of here."

Finley Forest is a quiet apartment complex on the outskirts of Chapel Hill where many graduate students live. *Author's collection.*

The tension on Summerwalk Circle was broken by tragedy on a Friday afternoon in February 2015. *Author's collection.*

As usual, he was mad about the parking spaces. He was yelling at Deah as Yusor watched the confrontation from the door of their kitchen. Hicks had a gun in his belt, as he usually did when he wanted to intimidate them. Suddenly, as he was dressing Deah down about the parking spaces, he pulled out his pistol and shot Deah several times in the chest. Yusor and Razan screamed as Hicks moved past the fallen body of Deah and moved toward them. He shot Yusor in the hip as he walked and then again in the head as she fell to the ground. Then he stood over Razan and shot her in the head as she begged, "Please, please." On his way out, Hicks shot Deah in the head once more for good measure. He tucked his weapon back in his belt and drove away from the scene.

When the police arrived, they soon found out who they were looking for. Craig Hicks was a forty-six-year-old former auto parts salesman and current student at Durham Technical Community College who was studying to be a paralegal. He had been married twice and was known in the neighborhood for being a very rude and aggressive man. Upon investigation, it became clear that Hicks was an avowed atheist and hated all forms of religion. He was critical of all faiths on his social media profiles, and his ex-wife told police that he was a huge fan of the film *Falling Down*, which portrays a man reaching his breaking point and going on a rampage. Neighbors said that he was militant about the parking in the neighborhood. He would yell at anyone who parked in the neighborhood without a parking sticker for the community and would often come out of his house to yell at someone if he thought their radio was too loud or if they were just bothering him in some way. Hicks had what one of his neighbors referred to as "equal opportunity anger." But where he had anger for seemingly everyone, he also seemed just a bit angrier at the young Muslim couple who lived there.

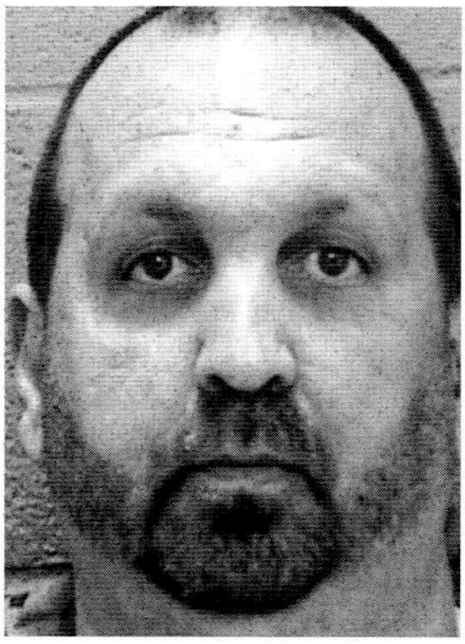

Craig Hicks. *Mugshot.*

The police did not have to look for Hicks long. He turned himself in to deputies in Pittsboro, North Carolina. He was taken into custody, and although the killer of the young students had been arrested, the question of why this had occurred was just beginning to be answered. The murders made police question whether they were indeed committed over a parking dispute, as Hicks had told the police when he turned himself in. Although Hicks had been an obstinate man to almost everyone, there were certainly concerns that he had a higher level of vitriol for his victims due to their religion. The murders reached national headlines and even prompted a candlelight vigil on the night of the murders at the Pit on the campus of UNC.

The next morning, there was a statement about the murders issued by President Barack Obama:

> *Yesterday, the FBI opened an inquiry into the brutal and outrageous murders of Yusor Mohammad Abu-Salha, Deah Shaddy Barakat and Razan Mohammad Abu-Salha in Chapel Hill, North Carolina. In addition to the ongoing investigation by local authorities, the FBI is taking steps to determine whether federal laws were violated. No one in the United States of America should ever be targeted because of who they are, what they look like or how they worship. Michelle and I offer our condolences to the victims' loved ones. As we saw with the overwhelming presence at the funeral of these young Americans, we are all one American family. Whenever anyone is taken from us before their time, we remember how they lived their lives—and the words of one of the victims should inspire the way we live ours. "Growing up in America has been such a blessing," Yusor said recently. "It doesn't matter where you come from. There's so many different people from so many different places, of different backgrounds and religions—but here, we're all one."*

Craig Hicks has maintained that he killed Deah, Yusor and Razan over the parking dispute, but this can never be known for sure. His true motives can be left to speculation, but it is an absolute truth that the murders were senseless and barbaric. In June 2019, Hicks was sentenced to three life sentences after finally pleading guilty to the murders and excepting punishment. His crime brought the federal hate crime charge into full debate, and although he was not charged with a hate crime in addition to the murders, the debate has brought the use of the hate crime legislation into the public conscience.

BIBLIOGRAPHY

Books

Athas, D., and W. Blythe. *Chapel Hill in Plain Sight: Notes From the Other Side of the Tracks*. Hillsborough, NC: Eno Publishers, 2010.

Emery, S.W. *Blood on the Old Well*. Dallas, TX: Prospect House, 1963.

Gaskin, N. *Time of Death: The True Tale of a Quest for Justice in 1960s Chapel Hill*. Chapel Hill, NC: Lystra Books & Literary Services, 2013.

Kotch, Seth. *Lethal State: A History of the Death Penalty in North Carolina*. Chapel Hill: University of North Carolina Press, 2019.

Newspapers

Chapel Hill Ledger
Chapel Hill News
Daily Tar Heel
Durham Morning Herald
Herald-Sun
North Carolinian
People's Press
Raleigh News and Observer
Statesville Daily Record

ABOUT THE AUTHOR

Rick Jackson is a native North Carolinian who grew up in Durham and now lives with his family in Wake Forest, just outside of Raleigh. He currently teaches business and economic courses to high school students after spending many years in banking and finance in various positions. He has always had a passion for history and the stories of the people who lived it. He holds a bachelor's degree in history from Campbell University and an MBA from the University of Mount Olive. Rick enjoys traveling around North Carolina with his wife, Meghan, and their three children, Savannah, Ricky and Charlotte.